YOU'RE OFF!

YOU'RE OFF!

The  Book of Red Cards

Adrian Besley

SIMON & SCHUSTER

London · New York · Sydney · Toronto · New Delhi

A CBS COMPANY

First published in Great Britain
by Simon & Schuster UK Ltd, 2012
A CBS Company

talkSPORT⚽

1 3 5 7 9 10 8 6 4 2

Simon & Schuster UK Ltd
1st Floor
222 Gray's Inn Road
London
WC1X 8HB

www.simonandschuster.co.uk

Simon & Schuster Australia
Sydney

Simon & Schuster India
New Delhi

A CIP catalogue for this book is available
from the British Library.

ISBN: 978-1-84983-947-1

Edited by Julian Flanders

Typeset and designed by Craig Stevens

Printed and bound in Italy by L.E.G.O. SpA

Contents

Introduction   8

Chapter 1
Set the Red Card Flying   9

Chapter 2
Once Upon a Time ...   15

Chapter 3
Walking For Your Country   22

Chapter 4
Your Cup Final – And You Mucked It Up   39

Chapter 5
What Happened Next?   58

Chapter 6
You're a Record Breaker!   71

Chapter 7
Who's the ****er in the Black?   86

Chapter 8
The Battle of ...   93

Chapter 9
Even the Best   102

Chapter 10
Eyes of the World   112

Chapter 11
You Did What?   128

Chapter 12
Serial Offenders   140

Chapter 13
The Greatest Ever Red Card   155

Acknowledgements and picture credits   160

▦ INTRODUCTION

Forget the last-minute goal, the goal-line clearance and the penalty shoot-out; the most dramatic moment of any match is when the man in black (or maroon or green) brandishes the dreaded red card. It can be heroic, tragic or comic, grotesque, bizarre or controversial; a moment of sheer joy, frustration or despair.

When the pious commentators drone on about 'an ugly side of the game we really don't want to see', or 'the referee ruining the game', the true fans rub their hands with glee and wait to see what happens next ... For this is football's drama within a drama. For a second, a minute – or sometimes even longer – the stage darkens and the spotlight is turned on the referee and a lone player – like a dueting couple coming to front of stage in a West End musical.

The other players, the spectators or the millions watching on TV, realise this is a pivotal moment. What will happen next? Does he accept his punishment meekly or flip out? Does the team fall to pieces or heroically prevail? Or does the man with the whistle go on a card-toting spree? Anything can happen and – as you will see – often does.

From dog-muck-strewn Sunday league pitches to state-of-the-art stadiums we find the brutal, the unbelievable, the hysterically funny and some forgotten gems. There are the iconic (remember Cantona's kung-fu attack or Di Canio pushing referee Paul Durkin over?), the serial offenders (21 reds in a career!) and the record-breakers, including 36 red cards in one match!

In the history of football there have been thousands of dismissals and each of them has its own story. Although this book is by no means an exhaustive list, hopefully it'll bring back a few memories, raise some smiles or even some long-forgotten ire – and if your interest stretches to wanting to see the incident again, many of the best can still be found on online.

Adrian Besley
London, July 2012

1

SET THE RED CARD FLYING

→ • • • • • • • • • • • • • • • •

'That's a red!' The red card, shorthand
for a dismissible offence, is an integral
part of football and has been taken
up by other sports, schools and
even some police departments.
But before the dramatic brandishing
of this feared piece of cardboard
was introduced, all that spectators,
commentators and players had to
go on was the referee's raised arm.
'What now?' they'd wonder. Is he
stretching, pointing out an interesting
feature of an Archibald Leitch stadium
or preparing for a future role in
Saturday Night Fever?

9

▦ RED FOR GO!

Ken Aston officiated in the 1962 World Cup finals in Chile, taking charge of the notorious game between Chile and Italy (see page 101), a match in which armed police officers had to come on to the pitch to help him keep control. Then, four years later, as chairman of FIFA's refereeing committee, Aston was overseeing the World Cup quarter-final between England and Argentina at Wembley (see pages 77–9), and had to usher the dismissed Argentinian captain Rattin off the field. The feeling that both incidents had been inflamed by

Ken couldn't help feeling there was something missing from his 'You're off!' signal.

the lack of a common language between players and officials was already nagging away at the über-referee's rulebook of a brain.

On the morning following the Argentina game the two famous Charlton brothers, Jack and Bobby, were in bed reading the Sunday newspapers' reports of the game. Jack was surprised to discover that, apparently, he had received a caution and even more astounded to find out his goody-two-shoes brother had been booked, too. 'Me? Never!' replied the balding never-ever-booked-in-my-life striker. So they rang FIFA, where Aston picked up the phone to confirm that they had, in fact, both been cautioned.

Later Aston was driving home through Kensington in his swish MG sports car and got caught in a series of traffic lights. The transgressions of Rattin and the Charlton brothers whirled through his mind as he impatiently tapped his fingers on the steering wheel and it suddenly came to him: '... Yellow, take it easy; red, I'm off. I thought, well, this is the way to overcome the language problem in international matches.'

FIFA liked his idea of a yellow card for a caution and a red for a dismissal, and the system was introduced for the next World Cup, in Mexico. Amazingly, no one was sent off during that particular tournament, but the little card would more than make its impact in matches and tournaments to come.

▦ 'WHAT HAS VAN BOMMEL GOT TO DO TO GET A RED CARD?'

Well, to answer Clive Tyldesley's continual vuvuzela-like howl during his 2010 World Cup final commentary on ITV, we need to refer to FIFA's Laws of the Game and in particular the section of Rule 10 that refers to Sending-off Offences. Here we discover that 'a player, substitute or substituted player is sent off if he commits any of the following seven offences':

◥ Serious foul play
How 'serious'? Might a really miserable long throw count?

⚡ Violent conduct
Nothing here about 'studs up', 'the precise angle of the elbow before it entered the eye socket' or 'two-feet clearly off the ground there, Dave?'

⚡ Spitting at an opponent or any other person
We're looking at you Mr Diouf – with notable mention to Frank Rijkaard (see pages 119–120).

⚡ Denying the opposing team a goal or an obvious goalscoring opportunity by deliberately handling the ball (this does not apply to a goalkeeper within his own penalty area).
See the textbook example performed by Uruguay's Luis Suarez against Ghana in the 2010 World Cup (see pages 138–39), an act for which he was chaired off the pitch by his teammates.

⚡ Denying an obvious goalscoring opportunity to an opponent moving towards the player's goal by an offence punishable by a free kick or a penalty kick
'Obvious'? Are we talking 'obvious' to Lionel Messi or to Darren Bent?

⚡ Using offensive, insulting or abusive language and/or gestures
Cue Messrs Allardyce, Warnock, Holloway et al spouting forth about the factory floor, it's a man's game etc and Fergie defending Rooney for shouting his favourite profanity at a million kids down a TV camera ...

⚡ Receiving a second caution in the same match
For 'Well, I thought the first yellow was pretty harsh' read 'my thick-as-pig-muck, hack-anything-that-moves midfielder was too stupid to remember he'd already been booked ...'

▦ 'I DEED NOT ZEE ZE INCIDENT'

Arsenal have received 56 Premier League red cards during Arsène Wenger's tenure as manager. He admitted that Jack Wilshere's red in a match against Birmingham in October 2010 was probably

Wenger's eyesight problems often means he mistakes officials for his players ...

justified, but the rest he has taken issue with or just not seen. Here are his five best red card reactions:

'[Emmanuel Petit] wanted to protect himself as the referee was running his way.' Petit was banned for three games for pushing Paul Durkin as he claimed a handball (v. Aston Villa, October 1997).

'We are not a dirty side. In fact we are a nice side, too nice at times.' Petit received Arsenal's 19th red card in less than two and a half seasons under Wenger (v. Wolves, January 1999).

'Red cards are not inevitable but it is something to do with the size of our pitch. At home it is tighter.' So it's not the refs, it's the pitch. Arsenal had five red cards at home that season – and five away! (2001–02).

'The first yellow card was very harsh. I didn't see the second one.' The classic Wenger defence is wheeled out yet again, as he was the only person in the stadium that missed Emmanuel Eboue lashing out at Spurs' Luka Modric (February 2009).

'When they brought on Frei they looked for a second yellow card on Djourou and they got it.' Wenger accuses Martin Jol of deliberately getting his defender sent off – by bringing on a tricky winger! (v. Fulham, January 2012).

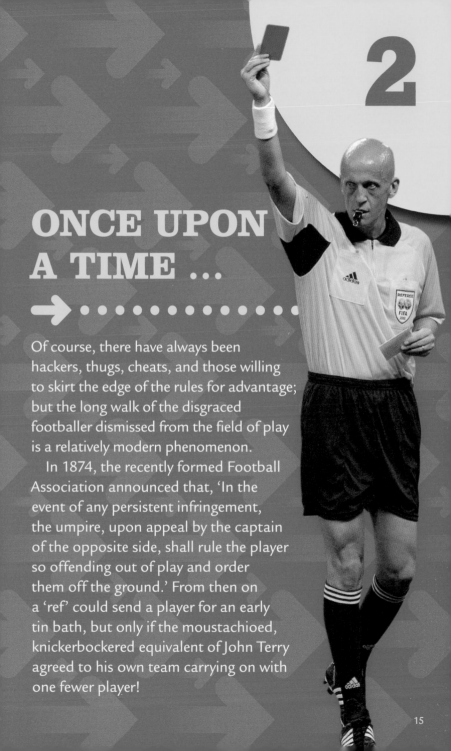

2

ONCE UPON A TIME ...

→ ● ● ● ● ● ● ● ● ● ● ● ● ● ● ●

Of course, there have always been hackers, thugs, cheats, and those willing to skirt the edge of the rules for advantage; but the long walk of the disgraced footballer dismissed from the field of play is a relatively modern phenomenon.

In 1874, the recently formed Football Association announced that, 'In the event of any persistent infringement, the umpire, upon appeal by the captain of the opposite side, shall rule the player so offending out of play and order them off the ground.' From then on a 'ref' could send a player for an early tin bath, but only if the moustachioed, knickerbockered equivalent of John Terry agreed to his own team carrying on with one fewer player!

In 1885, football became an openly professional game and all pretentions to gentlemanly conduct and friendly amateurism went out the window. However, it took another four years for the FA to get tough ... well, tough-ish. From 1889, the now sole arbiter, a referee, was given the power to send a player off in the event that he had already been cautioned and then re-offended or had committed a single act of 'violent conduct'.

The early professional clubs were soon recording their first dismissals: William 'Dundee' Robertson walked for Sheffield United in the Sheffield County Cup final replay in March 1890; Jack Evans was registered as taking Stoke's first early bath at Everton in November 1892, and in 1894 West Bromwich Albion hero Billy Bassett was their first to go – ordered off for 'unparliamentary language' in a match against Millwall.

Of course, once the gloves came off, the win-at-all-cost attitude settled in for a long and bumpy ride, giving rise to some astonishing dismissals.

THE COTTON MILL RUCKUS

Local derby encounters were already a source of blood and thunder. The Cotton Mill Derby – Burnley versus Blackburn Rovers – involved two of the original members of the Football League. Rovers had mullered their Lancashire rivals in every game of the first three league seasons. But with Rovers' England centre-forward Jack Southworth, who scored goals for fun (including 12 in ten matches between the sides), on the wane, Burnley sensed their chance.

At Turf Moor on 12 December 1891, in front of thousands of flat caps and smouldering Woodbines, the teams came out to play in driving snow and howling gales. For once it was the home side that showed up. Perhaps mindful of the 6-1 hammering they'd received last time their neighbours had visited, they shot into a three-goal lead by half-time.

Rovers delayed their appearance for the second half for as long as possible. When they finally did reappear an altercation soon broke out and, as a result, Blackburn's Joe Lofthouse and Burnley's Alex

Stewart received their orders to leave the field. Taking exception to the punishment of Lofthouse, and possibly anticipating the warmth of the dressing room, Rovers' outfield players decided to follow him – every one of them.

This left the entire Burnley side to take on Rovers' goalkeeper, Herbie Arthur. According to which report you read, Arthur either claimed for offside as the Burnley players bore down on his goal, or picked up the ball and refused to take a goal kick. Either way, the ref decided that the game could not continue, abandoned the match and awarded the points to Burnley.

▦ THE DAY THEY STOPPED BIG BEN

What do you have to do to be banned from football for life? The last British footballer to receive a life ban didn't test positive for drugs, take a bribe or attack a ref; Willie Woodburn was stopped from playing after being sent off four times in his career – that's the same as that well-known hatchet man Gareth Barry. Woodburn is remembered as being one of the more classy defenders of his era, but with a short fuse, a hard tackle and an intense dislike of being kicked himself. However, he encountered a Scottish FA who insisted on acting like some kind of military junta.

'Big Ben' as the Ibrox Faithful christened him, was a member of Rangers 'Iron Curtain' defence for ten years until 1948 (when he was 29) before receiving his first ever dismissal – for a 'violent exchange' with Motherwell's Dave Mathie. And, it would be nearly another five years before his next expulsion – when he took a swing (and missed) at Clyde's Billy McPhail. But the SFA had Willie's card marked and seemed out to get him.

It was an unlikely Rangers rivalry with Stirling Albion – a series of matches that for some reason had a brutal undercurrent – that brought Big Ben's downfall. In September 1953, Stirling's McBain raised his fists to Woodburn and received a Glasgow kiss in repayment. Willie was suspended for six weeks and warned by the Scottish FA that 'a very serious view will be taken of any subsequent action.'

The subsequent action arrived almost a year later – against the very same opposition. Willie, nursing a knee injury, had seen all but a minute of the game out without further aggravation, despite the attentions of Stirling's Alec Paterson. Then, as Willie won a tackle, the young centre-forward locked his limbs around the strapped-up leg. As the two squared up to each other, Willie once again dropped the nut.

The SFA's disciplinary hearing a month later lasted barely four minutes: Woodburn was suspended *sine die* (indefinitely). Rangers seemed unwilling to fight the ban and Woodburn himself loved the club so much, he refused to kick up trouble, preferring to sit it out. He would wait three years for the punishment to be revoked, but by that time, Willie was 37 and had hung up his boots.

For his services to Latin. Big Ben (right) would make sure every Scottish schoolboy knew the meaning of the words *Sine Die*.

England great Tom Finney called it a grave injustice – and he wasn't wrong. The career of one of Scotland's finest ever players' careers had been terminated by a vindictive bunch of blazer-wearing idiots.

▦ STEEL CITY SHAKEDOWN

James A. Catton was the foremost football writer of those early years and it is thanks to him we have such great records of the Sheffield derby games of February 1900. Sheffield United and Sheffield Wednesday had fought out a 1-1 draw at Bramall Lane in the second round of that season's FA Cup. The match had been marred by a series of nasty tackles, so before the replay at Hillsborough, referee John Lewis went to the dressing room to warn the players to watch their behaviour.

Despite Lewis's efforts, Catton went on to describe a match he regarded as one of the roughest in history: 'the tie had not been long in progress when a Wednesday man was sent to the dressing room for jumping on to an opponent. Soon after that The Wednesday's centre-forward had his leg broken, but that was quite an accident. No blame attached to anyone. Another Wednesday player was ordered out of the arena for kicking an opponent … With two men in the pavilion reflecting on the folly of behaving brutally and another with a broken leg, it is no wonder that The Wednesday lost the tie.'

▦ THE ORIGINAL HARDMEN

Ah, those were the days, when defenders tackled properly and lily-livered forwards lived in fear of the next tackle putting them in a wheelchair for the rest of their lives. Before the 1970s clampdown, it was virtually 'anything goes' as long as you ended up with the ball. Goalkeepers, in particular, bore the brunt of the brutality. Until 1894 if a goalkeeper caught the ball it was legal for the attackers to barge him over the goal line – so much for the 'car-alarm' protection refs give today's keepers.

Hard-tackling, blood-and-thunder players could spread terror week in, week out and maintain a spotless disciplinary record. Take Arsenal and England's Wilf Copping, nicknamed the Iron Man. His catchphrase was 'the first man in a tackle never gets hurt' and proved as much in his man-of-the-match display against Italy in the Battle of Highbury in November 1934. Wilf went through his whole career without ever receiving a caution, let alone a dismissal.

It was, however, possible to get sent off – and many did. So here we find our first-ever serial offenders ...

Frank Barson

Yorkshireman Frank Barson signed as a professional footballer with Barnsley in 1911 after training as a blacksmith. It's sometimes said that he learned his rough style at Oakwell, but even before he could make his debut for the Tykes he had to serve a two-month suspension following a punch-up in a pre-season friendly against Birmingham City. His unique mix of a combative, aggressive style with a quick temper would often prove too much even in those laissez-faire days.

Although records are sometimes patchy, it is thought Barson was sent off 12 times over the next 20 years in a career that took him to Aston Villa, Manchester United, Watford and Wigan. In the 1920 FA Cup final he was singled out by referee Jack Howcroft before the match had even kicked off. Howcroft made a special trip to the dressing room to say, 'The first wrong move you make Barson, off you go.'

In Manchester he became notorious for the 'Barson Barge'. One such challenge, which knocked Manchester City's Sam Cowan flat out, led to Frank being banned for two months. On his debut for Watford, he received an early caution only to see a teammate later dismissed with the words 'Off you go, Barson.' He'd got away with that one but, after just a handful of games, he was sent off for kicking out at a Fulham player. The FA threw the book at him, suspending him for six months.

Despite a 5,000-strong petition against this draconian punishment, he never pulled a Hornets shirt on again. Instead, he ended his career kicking people for Wigan Borough. On Boxing Day 1930, at the age of 39 Frank played his last game for them against Accrington Stanley. In the 83rd minute he received his marching orders for assaulting an opponent.

Ernie Hart

Wayne Rooney reckons he was hard done by for getting a two-match ban for screaming obscenities down the nation's TV screens, but he should think himself lucky he wasn't playing 80 years earlier ...

In 1930 Leeds United's Ernie Hart was regarded one of the best centre-halves in the country. Winning his fifth cap, Hart starred in England's 4-3 defeat of Austria's 'Wunderteam' (unbeaten in 19 matches before that Stamford Bridge encounter) in 1932, but his international career would be cut short.

In April 1933, in the West Riding Senior Cup final against Huddersfield, Ernie was dismissed for swearing at the referee. The FA showed no mercy. He received a 28-day suspension, but his real punishment was to be left out of the England squad set to visit Italy and Switzerland the following month. Despite eventually being recalled to the national side, the suspension hung over him like a bad smell and Ernie would win just three more caps during his career.

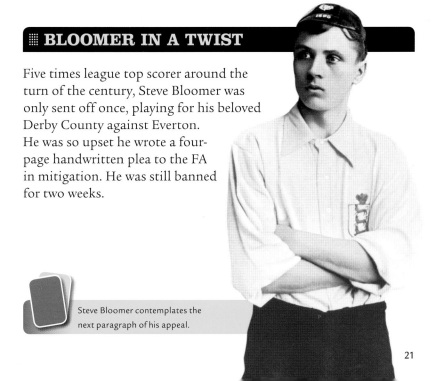

▦ BLOOMER IN A TWIST

Five times league top scorer around the turn of the century, Steve Bloomer was only sent off once, playing for his beloved Derby County against Everton. He was so upset he wrote a four-page handwritten plea to the FA in mitigation. He was still banned for two weeks.

Steve Bloomer contemplates the next paragraph of his appeal.

WALKING FOR YOUR COUNTRY

→ • • • • • • • • • • • • •

It's not quite the ultimate sacrifice you can make for your country, but taking a red for the Three Lions must be up there. It takes a brave player to go that extra yard (or 30 yards to the dressing room), under the full glare of the nation, which is why this hall of shame features such a select band.

3

It took until 1968 – 423 matches and 96 years – for England to have a man sent off in an international. Over the next 30 years – 749 matches – just three more received their marching orders, a record that stood second to none among the major footballing nations of the world.

Of course, it was too good to last. In just over a year, beginning with David Beckham's famous exit in France in the 1998 World Cup, England would double that total including: the first England player to be dismissed on home soil, earning the worst disciplinary record of any team in the Euro 2000 qualifiers, and, for the first time, having players sent off in (three) consecutive seasons. Since then they have settled into a pattern of one ejection every two years – a figure Wayne Rooney seems single-handedly intent on maintaining.

In total, England have had to play out over 400 minutes (the equivalent of four matches) with ten men. In this time they have failed to score, but have conceded only three goals (and one of those was a penalty after Rob Green's dismissal in a World Cup qualifier against Ukraine).

The Lions of Shame

Alan Mullery: v. Yugoslavia, 1968
Alan Ball: v. Poland, 1973
Trevor Cherry: v. Argentina, 1977
Ray Wilkins: v. Morocco, 1986
David Beckham: v. Argentina, 1998
Paul Ince: v. Sweden, 1998
Paul Scholes: v. Sweden, 1999
David Batty: v. Poland, 1999
Alan Smith: v. Macedonia, 2002
David Beckham: v. Austria, 2005
Wayne Rooney: v. Portugal, 2006
Rob Green: v. Ukraine, 2010
Wayne Rooney: v. Montenegro, 2011

::: THE FIRST CARD IS THE CRUELLEST

England managed to play a remarkable 423 games without having a player sent off, but on 5 June 1968 the first ever Lion was to get his marching orders. Clever money might have gone on the sometimes-shocking Norman Hunter or hard-tackling Jackie Charlton, the fiery Alan Ball or the 'uncompromising' Nobby Stiles to get there ahead of the rest, but the honour of the first international early bath falls to hard-working but unexceptional midfielder Alan Mullery.

As England faced up to Yugoslavia in a European Championship semi-final in Italy, Mullery, winning his 11th cap, found an opposition ready to resort to every underhand trick possible. In his autobiography, *Mullery*, the player himself recalled: 'Bobby Moore played a pass to me and an assassin called Trivic, who had been kicking lumps out of us the whole game, went right down the back of my legs with his studs. I cracked and, with the referee only five yards away, kicked him straight in the groin.'

Ironically it was Nobby Stiles, perhaps relieved to have escaped the ignominy of breaking the national team's disciplinary duck himself, who led Mullers off to the dressing room. Fearfully, Mullery awaited the wrath of England's stiff-lipped manager, Sir Alf Ramsey. 'Alf came in – I was expecting the biggest roasting – he shouted, "If you hadn't done it, I would have!"' The England boss even paid the £50 fine the player received.

The Tottenham midfielder hadn't completely escaped scot-free, however. Back at the hotel, he received a phone call from his wife. The message was short but to the point: you're a disgrace to the family! And, of course, the press went to town. This was not how an Englishman behaved on the pitch.

Had Mullery learned his lesson? No. A year later, he also became the second player to be sent off for the Three Lions. Preparing for the 1970 World Cup finals, England played a Mexico XI in Guadalajara (later to be the venue of their epic tie against Brazil). During a second-half melee, England's bad boy roughly manhandled a Mexican and once again paid the ultimate penalty. As it was in a friendly it didn't officially count, but nevertheless this time Sir Alf was not so supportive, saying, 'You just can't keep your nose out of things, can you?'

He did, however, continue to select Alan Mullery for the World Cup matches (the midfielder would score his only international goal in the famous quarter-final against West Germany) and the player went on to win 35 caps in all.

▦ AN OFF THE BALL INCIDENT

At 21, Alan Ball was the youngest member of England's World Cup-winning side and, according to fellow midfielder Nobby Stiles, was 'the best player on the pitch by far' in the 1966 final. A battling right midfielder who played with socks around his ankles, Ball had boundless energy, a great motor ... you get the picture, he ran around a lot.

Along with Billy Bremner, Ball helped maintain the stereotype of the short-tempered redhead, his squeaky high-pitched whines being heard even above the noise of the huge crowds that attended matches during the 1960s and 1970s. As early as his first season as a professional at Blackpool in 1963-64, Alan had set out his stall. He was sent off twice. First he got into a scrap with Denis Law, claiming in his autobiography to have riled the great Scot by saying, 'You're finished, you're old, step aside.' Then, having served a seven-match suspension, he was dismissed again for fighting, this time at Fulham, having already netted a hat-trick.

By 1965, at the age of 19, Ball had made his England debut and was virtually an ever-present in the side right through the 1966 and 1970 World Cups. But, crucially, he would miss England's final, decisive and ultimately disastrous qualifier against Poland in 1973. He was suspended after getting sent off against the same opponents in Chorzów.

England were frustrated, playing badly and 2-0 down in the 67th minute when a scramble left Martin Peters on the ground. Seeing the Polish player Cmikiewicz trying to kick his mate in the face brought the red mist down on Ball. He grabbed the midfielder by the throat with both hands and for good measure kneed him in the groin. A lesson others could learn: if you going to get sent off, make it worthwhile ...

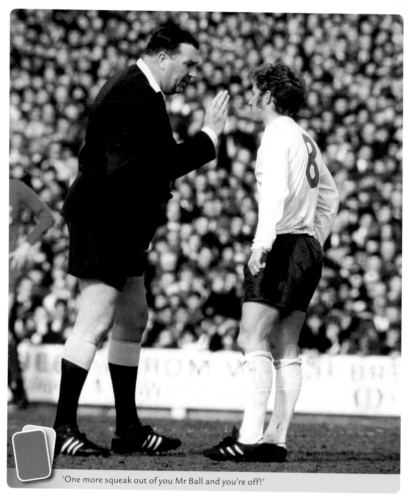

'One more squeak out of you Mr Ball and you're off!'

When Don Revie took over in 1974, Ball was made captain and in the last of a six-game run enjoyed a 5-1 thrashing of Scotland. But come the start of the next season his name was not even in the squad list – he had run his heart out for his country, but was shabbily discarded.

▦ ENGLAND LOSE THEIR CHERRY

Although he was sent off in a friendly, as this was against Argentina in Buenos Aires, there wasn't much friendliness in evidence that day either on the pitch or in the stands ...

Trevor Cherry, gritty defender and graduate of the 1970s Leeds United school of hard knocks, had made his international debut in March 1976 under his mentor Don Revie. The following summer, with the tough-tackling Cherry slotting in alongside other battlers like Emlyn Hughes, Phil Neal, Dave Watson and Brian Talbot, a distinctly uncompromising England team set off for a mini tour of South America – ideal preparation for the following year's World Cup finals.

In the heat of Buenos Aires' Bombonera in June 1977, the brave Lions faced a blossoming Argentina side containing Ossie Ardiles, Daniel Passarella, Alberto Tarantini – as well as the marvellously named Daniel Killer. A Stuart Pearson goal after just three minutes put the hosts in the worst possible mood and, with 60,000 spectators becoming increasingly hostile, the game settled into a niggly and bad-tempered tone.

Despite winger Daniel Bertoni's equaliser after a quarter of an hour, the rough tackling and off-the-ball offences grew increasingly nasty. Nevertheless, 51 minutes had passed without Uruguayan referee Ruiz reaching for the cardboard. Then Trev, with a tackle no worse than many that had passed during the game, took out Bertoni from behind.

The Argentinian goalscorer exacted his own retribution with a right hook to the defender's mouth and Ruiz finally went to his pocket – quickly dispatching Bertoni and then, with the crowd howling, seemed to decide the safest option was to order the bloodied Cherry to follow him off the pitch.

Cherry lost two teeth, Bertoni to this day bears the teeth-marks on his knuckles and England were left with a 1-1 draw, having taken another few steps down the dark alley of Anglo-Argentine relations. A year later, just down the road, Argentina were being crowned World Champions with Bertoni scoring their third goal in the final against the Netherlands. England, for all Revie's meticulous planning, had forgotten one small element – qualification.

As for Trevor – he avoided any further punishment and continued to play for England until 1980, winning 27 caps. However, after this game it was said he always needed two bites at the Cherry ...

▦ RAY WILKINS GETS BUTCH

In the words of Frank Sinatra, 'It happened in Monterrey, a long time ago ...' Some say the responsibilities of captaincy bring out a more mature approach in a player – but Ray Wilkins, an otherwise level-headed chap, proved the opposite can be true as well. Back when he was plain old Butch, Ray Wilkins would captain his country for a little over 60 seconds before getting his marching orders in the 1986 World Cup finals.

England had set off to Mexico with high hopes. In their number were Bryan Robson, Captain Marvel himself; Glenn Hoddle, the finest player of his generation; his partner in song Chris Waddle; goal machine Gary Lineker; and one of the best keepers ever in Peter Shilton. But in the heat of Monterrey they wilted almost immediately, losing 1-0 to a nondescript Portugal.

So, when skipper Robson went off with the usual gippy shoulder after 42 agonising goalless minutes of the next match with Morocco, many fans watching TV at home in England were changing channel to watch *Beadle's About*. But hey, Ray 'The Crab' Wilkins had taken the captain's armband – maybe things were about to turn around. Not exactly. A minute later, Butch, angry at not getting a free-kick, tossed the ball in the direction of the referee – a little too accurately, a little too powerfully. A second yellow meant 10-man England still had 45 minutes to play in the sapping South American heat.

In one of those footballing twists of fate, the exit of the two captains did change England's fortunes. Having hung on for a draw in the Morocco game, England were forced to change their attitude – and with Reid and Hodge replacing Robson and Wilkins, they suddenly looked like a team. They steamrollered Poland to qualify for the knockout stages, smashed Paraguay and found themselves in the quarter-finals against a Maradona-inspired Argentina. But that's another story ...

As for Wilkins – he earned a brief recall in the Euro qualifiers that November, but after 84 caps it was time to concentrate on a 'super' media career – and to finally drop the 'Butch' from his byline.

▦ NEVER MIND, HIS HAIR LOOKED NICE

England v. Argentina
World Cup, Second Round, St Etienne, France, 1998

'Simeone went down as if he'd been shot. My first thought was, "I've made a big mistake here."' David Beckham

Before St David, before LA David, even before Goldenballs, there was David Beckham, a 23-year-old who let his country down. Left out of Glenn Hoddle's original World Cup 1998 team for being too unfocused (possibly the manager's shorthand for 'on the phone to Posh all the time'), Becks had forced his way into the side by the time England met bitter rivals Argentina. When his perfectly weighted through-ball sent Michael Owen away to put England 2-1 up, it seemed the South Americans would struggle to contain their partnership. Even when Argentina equalised just before the break, most of those watching at home remained confident.

Then it all unravelled. They had been back on the field for just two minutes when Diego Simeone's clumsy challenge from behind took Beckham's legs away. For good measure he dug his hand into Beck's recently healed back and ruffled his hair. Which of these David took exception to has never been made clear, but in response the prostrate figure flicked his leg up and caught the backward-stepping Argentinian skipper – right in front of referee Kim Milton Nielsen.

Few questioned the subsequent red card, but has anyone ever been dismissed for such a namby-pamby, cissy strike? He might as well have laid his assailant out with a right hook. The myth – certainly apocryphal – tells how, as England's would-be hero sat distraught in the dressing room, his phone rang. Victoria listened to his woes of how he'd let his side down but comforted him in the only way she knew how, saying, 'Still, your hair looked nice, babe!'

As England fought a valiant rearguard action with 10 men, clung on to a draw and, of course, went out on penalties, the hordes back home had a ready-made scapegoat. '10 Heroic Lions, One Stupid Boy,' screamed the *Daily Mirror*, who handily included a Beckham dartboard for fans to 'take their fury out on'. A south London pub hung a Beckham effigy (well, a sack in a sarong – they didn't want to go to too much trouble) and distasteful comments were even made in the House of Commons.

It would be another three years – and an incredible performance against Greece that single-handedly won England a place at the next finals – before Becks could fully restore his reputation. Then, through World Cups, Olympic bids, international call-ups and snubs, he would never again (the Austrian aberration is easily overlooked) allow his dedication to the cause to be questioned.

▦ SCHOLES DROPS SOME GRENADES

Quite how Paul Scholes became, against Sweden in June 1999, the only England player ever to be sent off at Wembley is still a subject of debate. Not the manner of his going – two yellow cards which could have been red themselves – but what had driven him to charge around like a man with a time-bomb on his back from the outset?

Some blame England manager Kevin Keegan who, displaying his masterful tactical nous, had told the Manchester United midfielder to 'go out and drop a few grenades' in his pre-match wind-up speech. Others look to Scholes' previous appearance at Wembley, three months earlier, when he had notched a brilliant hat-trick against Poland. Was he trying to find that same buzz? And the less romantic will always point to the old chestnut: Paul Scholes can't tackle …

Is he a poor tackler? Or, as Arsène Wenger claimed, does the fiery Salford lad have a 'darker side'? The jury might still be out, but the match against Sweden could be exhibit A in the Professor's case. Despite being on a booking from the Poland match, Scholes immediately left any thoughts of caution behind as he clattered Hakan Mild in the very first minute with a crude two-footed challenge that could have earned him a red. Mild left the field minutes later with a nasty gash on his thigh.

With Scholes buzzing around like a headless chicken, it was only a matter of time before he earned a yellow card and his automatic one-match ban. A 28th-minute assault on the effective Stefan Schwarz was just the ticket. The half-time break having failed to calm him down, it took just six minutes for the midfielder to earn

Mr Misunderstood. Another well-intentioned but mis-timed tackle lands Paul Scholes in hot water.

his red ... taking out Schwarz again, this time just below the knee. The Wembley crowd seemed to breathe a sigh of relief that he had gone, but Scholes still left the pitch with an affronted look.

A 0-0 draw did nothing to enhance Keegan's stature as an international coach, but by remaining unbeaten in the next three qualifiers, England would face Scotland in the play-offs and go on to fail to impress in Euro 2000. Paul Scholes would continue as a mainstay of the national team, winning 66 caps, until he decided to quit in 2004. Despite begging from Eriksson and Capello, we'd see no more mistimed tackles or grenades from the Ginger Prince in an England shirt.

▦ WHAT A WINKER!

England v. Portugal

World Cup, quarter-final, Gelsenkirchen, Germany, 2006

You have to wonder about the English collective football brain sometimes. Having treated David Beckham like a latter-day Lord Haw Haw for a petulant snipe, only eight years had passed before Wayne Rooney was instantly forgiven for a far more serious offence and the blame was laid firmly at the eye of Cristiano Ronaldo.

Germany 2006, and England had once again reached a World Cup quarter-final. Topping a group comprising Trinidad and Tobago, Sweden and Paraguay, they had beaten Ecuador en route to a date with Portugal in Gelsenkirchen – but still nobody seemed too convinced about Sven-Göran Eriksson's boys.

The lack of creative inspiration that had stilted the team in every match was more than evident as England locked horns with Portugal, the side that had eliminated them from the Euros two years earlier. Fifty pretty uneventful minutes had elapsed when captain David Beckham limped off, but worse was to come just 10 minutes later as Rooney battled to keep possession from three Portugal defenders.

Ricardo Carvalho pulled at the fiery forward's shirt before falling over, at which point Rooney seemed to aim his foot at the Chelsea defender's groin. Of course, Carvalho reacted dramatically and the Portuguese surrounded referee Horacio Elizondo – Ronaldo to the fore. Calmly, the Argentinian in the black – who had sent Beckham off in the Club World Championship in 2000 – took Rooney aside, brandished the card and ignored his protests.

Ironically, the incident managed to achieve what Sven had pointedly failed to do – put some fire into English bellies. Despite temperatures close to 30 degrees, the 10 men created chances for Lennon, Terry and Crouch and Owen Hargreaves put in a man-of-the-match performance. Come penalties though and English hearts sank. We never win these, the fans complained – and the team didn't fail to disappoint as Lampard, Gerrard and Carragher all saw their efforts saved by Ricardo.

Rooney claimed to be 'gobsmacked' by the dismissal, but must have been more surprised by the reaction back home. The TV cameras had caught Ronaldo's sly wink to the Portuguese bench just after the dismissal. Caught you! The red card must have been a cunning plan orchestrated by Rooney's Manchester United teammate. Pundit Alan Shearer went so far as to suggest Rooney might 'stick one on him' when they got together in pre-season training.

Rooney was all too familiar with his teammate's evil scheme: 'Not the wink Cristiano, please. Anything but the wink.'

Years later Rooney still claims it was an accident, yet appreciates the fact that Ronaldo's wink deflected attention from his actions. 'Of course I was happy I didn't get what Becks got or even some of what Phil Neville suffered after Euro 2000.' Well, at least he learned his lesson ...

AN IDIOT ABROAD

It had been a long haul back from England's disappointing 2010 World Cup, but Fabio Capello took England to Montenegro needing just a point to book their ticket to the Euro 2012 finals. Two up after only 30 minutes, the FA big nobs were already scanning Trip Advisor for luxury suites in Poland and Ukraine. What could possibly go wrong?

Two words: 'Wayne' and 'Rooney'. Despite the distraction of his father facing criminal charges back home, the new 'mature' Rooney was playing a blinder. He made both goals and was creating havoc on and off the ball. Then, with just 18 minutes remaining, he flipped.

Maybe he couldn't face another set of deflating opening round group games at the finals; perhaps he felt his recent hair transplant hadn't had sufficient publicity. Whatever. The moment had arrived for Bad Wayne to emerge again – he kicked out against Miodrag Džudović for little apparent reason, leaving Wolfgang Stark reaching for the red.

Though England held on for a 2-2 draw and the required point, the focus was on Rooney. The *Guardian* wrote, 'It was a test of ... discipline. Rooney failed the exam comprehensively,' while other papers headlines concluded 'We will Roo this moment', 'Roo fool!' and 'Roonatic!'

Now the second-ever England player to receive two reds, Wayne wrote a nice apology letter to UEFA in his best handwriting, but still received a three-match ban – which would keep him out of all England's Euro 2012 group games.

As Peter Crouch and Jermain Defoe bought their England ties back from the charity shops, the FA, still merrily handing out similar three-match bans themselves, got down and begged. On appeal, UEFA reduced the ban from three matches to two, the France and Sweden games. Meanwhile Capello indicated that every friendly until then would be a desperate search for a team that could win *sans* Rooney ...

▦ THEY GIVE AS GOOD AS THEY GET

With 13 red cards, exactly the same total as England, Johnny Foreigner clearly dishes it out just as much as our homegrown bruisers. Here is a list of the guilty parties:

1 Manuel Grimaldo, Peru – May 1962, Lima, Peru. Grimaldo earns the honour of being the first player to be dismissed against England by swearing at the referee in a 4-0 defeat.

2 José Torres, Portugal – May 1964, São Paulo, Brazil. England played in a 'Little World Cup' tournament in Brazil. Having been soundly thrashed by Pelé's Brazil, England beat Portugal 4-3 after their striker José Torres (ironically nicknamed 'The Kind Giant') was sent off for trying to punch the referee after a goal had been disallowed for offside.

3 Antonio Rattin, Argentina – July 1966, Wembley. In the World Cup quarter-finals, Rattin became the first player ever to be sent off at the famous stadium (see pages 77–9).

4 Billy Ferguson, Northern Ireland – October 1966, Belfast. In England's first match as World Champions, winger Ferguson's challenge – sometimes reported as a 'kick up the arse' – on Alan Ball saw his dismissal in the 84th minute of this Home International match.

5 Alex Vencel, Czechoslovakia – October 1975, Bratislava, Czechoslovakia. The 2-1 reverse was Don Revie's first defeat as England boss, but the game is more memorable for the Czech substitute goalkeeper being sent off for arguing with the referee – from the bench!

6 Gilbert Dresch, Luxembourg – March 1977, Wembley. Dresch becomes just the second player ever to be sent off in a Wembley international as his team are hammered 5-0 by Keegan, Channon et al.

7 Daniel Bertoni, Argentina – June 1977, Buenos Aires, Argentina (see page 27). The winger gets the red for knocking Trevor Cherry's teeth out in a so-called friendly.

8 Tesuji Hashiratani, Japan – June 1995, Wembley. Japan nearly earned a draw in their first game against England. Only two minutes remained when their skipper's reaction goal-line punch kept out Gazza's acrobatic shot. Unfortunately he wasn't the keeper, and David Platt scored the winner from the spot.

9 Martin Petrov, Bulgaria – June 1999, Sofia, Bulgaria. The future Manchester City and Bolton winger was making his international debut.

Coming on as a replacement for his idol Hristo Stoichkov, he earned two yellows in just eight minutes, sobbing his heart out as he left the pitch.

10 Ronaldinho, Brazil – June 2000, Shizuoka, Japan. Eight minutes after David Seaman had watched Ronaldinho's 50th-minute free-kick sail into the net to put them 2-1 up, the Brazilian was walking off. A harsh call for a clumsy tackle on Danny Mills, but it barely mattered; Brazil just kept the ball to themselves for half an hour.

11 Bernt Haas, Switzerland – June 2004, Coimbra, Portugal. The West Brom defender was unluckily booked twice in 10 minutes in the Euro group game to allow England to stroll a 3-0 victory they really didn't deserve.

12 Robert Kovač, Croatia – September 2008, Zagreb, Croatia. Kovač viciously stuck the elbow on Joe Cole, saw red and the talented Croatians fell apart. A Theo Walcott-inspired thrashing ensued – the first time Croatia had lost at home.

13 Stephan Lichtsteiner, Switzerland – September 2010, Basle, Switzerland. The defender earned a second yellow card for a foul on James Milner on 64 minutes as our brave lads swept to a 3-1 win and a place at Euro 2012.

▦ PUTTING THE RED IN THE RED, WHITE AND BLUE (AND GREEN)

And what of the rest of the Britain? They too have a long and illustrious list of wrongdoers, miscreants and hard-done-by stories:

Northern Ireland

Back in 1966, Billy Ferguson (see page 35) staked his place as the first Northern Irishman to get his marching orders, but let's not forget mud-slinging George Best (pages 104–5), Mal Donaghy in the famous 1982 World Cup defeat of Spain and two teenagers: Ryan McGivern, sent off on his debut (page 56) and Adam Thompson, who walked in a humiliating 5-0 defeat to the Republic in 2011.

Special note, however, must go to Northern Ireland's top scorer David Healy for his performance against Wales at the Millennium Stadium in 2004. The tone of the match had been set as early as the eighth minute when Robbie Savage reacted to a Michael Hughes foul by trying to rip his shorts off. After the necessary handbags, both men were ordered off. Three minutes later Whitley put the visitors ahead, and after another 20 minutes Healy cheekily lobbed the Wales keeper and ran round him to nod home a second.

Understandably delighted, Healy headed for the corner, kicked the flag and pumped his arm in front of the Welsh fans. Finally heading back to his own half, the Preston striker was gobsmacked to find himself looking at the raised arm of Italian referee Domenico Messina. Healy had been given yellow cards for (1) kicking the flag and (2) celebrating in an over-exuberant fashion. Wales came back to draw the match and Healy wasn't even allowed to appeal. You can appeal only against straight reds!

Wales

It wasn't until 1973 that Wales registered on the red card record. Bearded, grafting winger Trevor Hockey (once nicknamed 'the Brum Beatle') earned the recognition for retaliation against midfielder Leslaw Ćmikiewicz in a 3-0 defeat in Poland. Hockey, who had earned nine caps and memorably scored in Wales' victory over Poland in Cardiff, would never play for his country again.

Trivia note 1: In 2001, Ryan Giggs, captaining Wales for the third time, was given the only red card in his career in a World Cup qualifier in Norway.

Trivia note 2: In September 2003 when Wales played Finland, West Brom's Jason Koumas picked up two yellow cards to become the first Wales player to be dismissed at the new Millennium Stadium (Arsenal's Francis Jeffers had been the first ever, just a month earlier, against Manchester United in the Community Shield).

Scotland

The Rest of Britain step aside – the Scots trampled the lot of them, getting a man into the early bath as far back as 1951. Dundee hero and one-time British record signing (£15,500 in 1947) Billy Steel became the first Scotland player to be sent off in May of that year. In a pitched battle masquerading as a football match, Scotland played Austria in Vienna. On seeing his skipper George Young get a right kicking, Billy took the law into his own hands and paid the ultimate penalty.

Celtic's Bertie Auld was the next to go. In 1959, he made it to the 93rd minute of his international debut, in a match against Holland, before being dismissed for retaliation, and two years later Paddy Crerand committed the same offence, this time against Czechoslovakia, to become the third. By 2012 they had reached 17 dismissals, more than any other home nation.

Among the good ones were: Richard Gough, who rose to blatantly catch a ball in a 1992 World Cup qualifier against Switzerland ('The ball hit a sprinkler head and just sort of popped up. I instinctively put my hands up and caught it.'); the only red card of battling Joe Jordan's career, a clash with Terry Boyle which left the Welshman with a broken nose and a missing tooth; and Andy Gray in his fourth international appearance, 'The old Scottish mist descended,' Andy recalls. 'The guy punched me and when the ball was down the other end I gave it to him back. Unfortunately, I was caught.'

Pride of place – and one of the most amusing dismissals ever – however, goes to Lisbon Lion Tommy Gemmell. As Scotland took on West Germany in Hamburg in 1969, Gemmell, at full stride, was taken out by midfielder Helmut Haller. Swivelling on a pfennig, Tommy started after the German, who instead of facing up to him, turned tail and legged it. Never lacking in pace, the Scot quickly caught him and delivered a well-earned scythe to his shins. Check out the hilarious re-creation of the incident on David Baddiel and Frank Skinner's *Fantasy Football* on YouTube.

YOUR CUP FINAL – AND YOU MUCKED IT UP

→ • • • • • • • • • • • • • • •

It's the big one – the cup final, the league decider or the grudge match against your local rivals. Perhaps it's your debut or the first game since your big-money move. You've played the game in your head and now all you need is to go out there and do it for real. So, how come you're back in the dressing room kicking the toilet door when the game's only 15 minutes old?

You can put it down to the tension, being too hyped up or the importance of the occasion getting to you, but when your teammates are watching the opposition lifting that trophy it's you they'll be thinking of – and not in a sympathetic way.

ON YOUR BIKEY

With seconds ticking away in injury time of a semi-final of the 2008 Africa Cup of Nations, Cameroon's Andre Bikey had one of football's great moments of madness, a rush of blood to the head that left him missing the final.

Bikey, who would go on to play for Reading and Burnley, had enjoyed a great game in the heart of Cameroon's defence as they led 1-0 against host nation Ghana. But, as his teammate Rigobert Song was being attended by medical staff, Bikey completely lost it.

The Ghanaian medical team were obviously desperate for their team to restart the match and needed to get the Cameroon skipper off the field as soon as possible. Song, understandably, was in no hurry. So when one of the medics attempted to help him aboard the motorised stretcher, Bikey decided to intervene. His shove on the luminous jacketed helper was enough to send the poor guy sprawling. The man with the cards, Abderrahim El Arjoun, had little option but to flash the red, forcing the defender to take the walk of shame accompanied by a shower of water bottles from the Ghanaian crowd.

Bikey would miss the biggest match of his career and Cameroon would miss their towering defender – they lost 1-0 to Egypt in the final.

IN THE DROG HOUSE

The 2008 Champions League final threw together Manchester United and Chelsea – the two best sides in England, the two richest sides in Europe and, possibly, the two most whining sets of players in the world. The match was gripping in its intensity, with United's early dominance and lead being countered by an equaliser and a surging second-half Chelsea performance.

Chelsea's eventual defeat in the penalty shoot-out might just have been bad luck. Skipper John Terry, who took the fateful fifth penalty, could have won it for the Londoners, but slipped as he took it and even then hit the post. However, bad luck isn't much of a story when there's a prize scapegoat around, so step forward Didier Drogba.

In the run-up to the game, Wayne Rooney (sounding somewhat like a pot discussing a kettle) alluded to Drogba, saying, 'Sometimes it seems as if his head's not quite there.' Yet it took until the 115th minute for the pasty-faced soothsayer's words to ring true. Just seconds after the players had sportingly helped heal opposition players' cramp agonies, a spat erupted over well, nothing really, and before you could say 'my Bentley's bigger than yours', Drogba was slapping Vidic and suffering the ignominious long walk.

Sent off with five minutes remaining of the match – is that such a crime? After all, he had nearly won the game with a spanking long-distance shot that just clipped the post. No. It was the consequences of the oh-so-likeable Ivorian seeing red that placed the blame for Chelsea's ultimate defeat at his feet.

The post-match finger ended up pointing in Drog's direction when it became clear that his red card had meant there was no fifth penalty taker. When no one else stepped forward to take the decider, it fell upon the skipper, Terry. 'John was not in the first five to take a kick, but things changed during the game,' said the Chelsea assistant manager Henk ten Cate. 'The sending-off of Drogba made us change it [the order].' Fair enough, guilty as charged, you might say. But wait a second! Who's that keeping his head low at the back? Nicolas Anelka – Drogba's partner in sulk.

Surely the sharp-shooting French goal machine who had cost Chelsea £15 million just months previously could have taken the fifth? Well, no actually. Anelka, who went on to miss the crucial sixth penalty, justified himself afterwards by asserting, 'I said, "No way. I came on practically as a full back and you want me to shoot a penalty?"' Of course, the poor mite, it would have been too much. It must all have been Drogba's fault then.

Of course, what goes around comes around, and Drogba would be back for his revenge a few years later.

▦ ON HIS WEMBLEY WAY

Everton v. Manchester United
FA Cup final, 1985

We had to sit through over 100 years of FA Cup finals before the first ever dismissal – despite matches like the notoriously rough 1913 final, which featured a feud between two players and 17 minutes of added time, the 1956 effort in which Peter Murphy broke Bert Trautmann's neck or the X-rated 1970 Chelsea v. Leeds epic. When it came, it was in a pretty dire match enlivened only by the sending off and Norman Whiteside's exquisite winner.

United for once had started as underdogs as Everton looked set to win the League and Cup Double and a European prize in the same season. After 78 minutes of uneventful football, a mistake by United's Paul McGrath launched an Everton counter-attack near the halfway line. When Peter Reid tried to offload the ball to an in-motion Andy Gray, he found his legs taken out from under him by Northern Irish international Kevin Moran.

Referee Peter Willis looked like he was only going to issue a caution, but presented the red card to the shocked defender, who went ballistic and the calm Frank Stapleton seemed to be the only thing stopping him throttling the retired police inspector.

Referee Willis threatens to blow his whistle really loud in Moran's ear if he doesn't leave the field.

Come the final whistle, Whiteside's curling effort proved to be the difference between the sides; at which point the debate turned to whether Moran would be entitled to a medal. He later told the *Observer*, 'United manager Ron Atkinson pulled me aside and said, "I just found out that you can't collect your medal. But you can go up the steps, you deserve that."' The next few days saw a concerted media campaign to find justice for the Manchester One and Moran finally did get his gold token.

Through 21st-century eyes, Moran's tackle was very late and he was the last defender – however, it was barely in the United half. He couldn't have quibbled with a yellow, but a red still seems pretty harsh.

THE CARD THAT CHANGED A GAME – WELL … SORT OF … MAYBE …

Barcelona v. Arsenal

Champions League, Round of 16, 2nd Leg, Camp Nou, March 2011
'We would have won that game,' the Arsenal manager raged after an onslaught at Camp Nou had seen Arsenal eliminated from the Champions League. 'I felt that, like in the first game, we would have come back into it and overall I am convinced we would have won this game.'

What had prevented his team taking victory against a side ranked by many as the world's greatest-ever club team was the dismissal of Arsenal's ace Robin van Persie. Until his ejection in the 55th minute, Arsenal were still in the tie with the aggregate score sitting at 1-1. OK, so they had managed only around 20 per cent possession and had barely managed to get into their opponents' half, let alone had a shot on target – but why let the facts ruin a bloody good excuse?

An exquisite chipped pass from Tomas Rosicky had finally pierced the Barca defence. With van Persie through on goal, it looked for a split-second like Arsenal might actually have a chance – only for the defenders to pull up and the referee's assistant to raise his flag for offside. Van Persie took a rare clumsy first touch and knocked a half-hearted effort a couple of yards wide of the post. A weak strike or time wasting – that was the question?

Massimo Busacca, the Swiss referee, instinctively knew, brandished both yellow and red cards at the striker and nonchalantly turned to resume the game. Van Persie, who had already been booked for roughing up Danny Alves, was stunned. Catching up with the ref he did an impressive charade. Three syllables? No, five words? The whole thing ... He hadn't heard the whistle!

Possibly Robin was right. Camp Nou was rocking and the volume was turned up. Even though both the defenders beside him seem to react as soon as the whistle went, maybe his concentration had led him to not hear the whistle or notice the flag. But his shot lacked conviction and his reaction was one of deep frustration rather than the anguish of a player who had cocked-up Arsenal's best chance of the evening. Either way it was a harsh second yellow in such a big game, made worse when (poor) substitute Nicklas Bendtner missed a gilt-edged chance late in the game – an away goal that would have trumped Barca's 3-2 aggregate advantage.

Wenger continued to lay it on thick, 'I think two kinds of people can be unhappy: those who love Arsenal and those who love football,' he said – forgetting who had really played the football in that match. Barca coach Guardiola hadn't, 'They did not have three passes in a row,' he reminded us.

▦ THE FOUR-MINUTE MATCH

Al-Ahly v. Zamalek

Cairo, Egypt, 1999

The Cairo derby – Al-Ahly against Zamalek – makes Old Firm encounters look like playground squabbles. The two best teams in Egypt, and indeed the whole of Africa, have massive followings throughout the Arab world and the derby result regularly decides the championship. So fierce is the rivalry that they import foreign referees (including Uriah Rennie in 2003) to ensure complete fairness.

In 1998-99 the derby fell on the penultimate weekend of the season. German World Cup referee Mark Batta had been called in to officiate, but for once few expected fireworks: Ahly, with 64 points to Zamalek's 50, had sealed the title long ago. The teams would just go through the motions. Or so they thought ...

The game began sedately enough, but after just four minutes Zamalek's Abdel-Aziz clattered into Al-Ahly defender Ibrahim Hassan. It was a rough challenge from behind and Batta had no hesitation in producing a red card. This might have raised eyebrows in the *Match of the Day* studios, but in the intense atmosphere generated by 40,000 fans at the neutral Cairo Stadium it caused mayhem.

While the Zamalek players surrounded the ref, coach Farouk Gaafar was already calling them off the pitch. They retreated to their dressing room, but after a few minutes seemed to be returning. Back on the pitch, however, they waved to their fans situated along one side of the stadium and disappeared back down the tunnel. Following FIFA rules to the letter, Batta waited 10 minutes then abandoned the match.

The Egyptian FA threw the book at Zamalek: fining the club £16,000, docking them nine points, suspending Gaafar and two 'ringleader' players. If that wasn't enough, three of the club's fans then decided to sue their own team for £180,000 in 'moral damages'.

▦ THE MULTIPLE-CHOICE FINAL

Arsenal v. Barcelona
Champions League final, Paris, 2006

Quite probably, Arsenal would never have reached their first ever Champions League final without the heroics of Jens Lehmann. He had kept a record 10 successive clean sheets on the way to the final, including an 88th-minute penalty save in the semi-final against Villarreal. Had the keeper not been dismissed in the final, maybe the records would have shown a Gunners win, but this is 'Mad Jens' (see pages 149–150) so there really is no saying ...

This was Barcelona mark one, pre-Messi but still a potent force orchestrated by Ronaldinho and spearheaded by Samuel Eto'o. And when, in the 18th minute, the Brazilian sent his striker clear, it was left to Lehmann to stop him. At the edge of the area, Eto'o tried to round the keeper, but found his ankle clipped by Lehmann's hand and tumbled to the ground.

The ball, however, was still in motion and Giuly duly obliged with a simple tap-in. Referee Terje Hauge, who had already blown for the foul, had a dilemma. Should he:

A) Give the goal and book or let off the keeper;

B) Award a free-kick and book the keeper;

C) Award a free-kick and send off the keeper?

Hauge chose option C but later admitted that if he'd had a minute to reflect then he would have opted for A with a booking – a decision that both teams claim they would have preferred. As it was, Lehmann walked, Robert Pires was sacrificed in what became his last ever performance for the Gunners and Manuel Almunia got to play in a European Cup final.

With 10 men Arsenal got to within 13 minutes of one of the great results in the history of the competition. Leading through Sol Campbell's first-half header, they soaked up the Barca pressure and looked dangerous on the break, with Thierry Henry missing a sitter of a chance to double their advantage. It took substitute Henrik Larsson to unlock the Gunners' resolute defence, setting up Eto'o for the equaliser and, just four minutes later, crossing for Belletti to slot home the winner.

While Wenger raged at the injustice (overlooking the disallowed goal), Lehmann was philosophical, 'He could have given advantage to Barcelona, but the referee had to make a very quick decision,' said the German international. And his effort had not been in vain – he did get in the record books as the first player ever to be sent off in a European Cup final.

▦ WEMBLEY, COVER YOUR EYES!

August 1974. For the first time ever Wembley was to host the FA Charity Shield, the showpiece season opener. It was also the first time for years that the league champions had actually faced the cup winners and, most importantly, it was a mouth-watering clash between the two clubs who dominated English football in those days. Bill Shankly would take charge of Liverpool for the last time and Brian Clough would begin his reign at Leeds – the very club he had consistently criticised for their dirty and unsporting behaviour.

Leeds' midfield enforcers Billy Bremner and Johnny Giles got straight to work, dishing out some meaty challenges. Then, when Giles got a taste of his own medicine with a clip on his ankle, he lashed out at the offender, earning a booking and a stiff lecture for his trouble. The main event, however, was still to come.

In the 61st minute Kevin Keegan was floored off the ball by Giles. Not knowing who had hit him, Keegan got up and took out his frustration on Billy Bremner, who had been on his case all afternoon and happened to be standing next to him. The redheaded Scottish ball of fire and the feather-cut future of English football traded punches before referee Jack Taylor (who had taken charge of the previous month's World Cup final) dismissed both players.*

The Times takes up the story, 'That, in itself, would have been enough to disgust. But both men compounded the felony as they

When 47 came up as the bonus ball that night, ref Jack Taylor was glad he'd got the players to turn round.

began the long walk to the dressing rooms by shamelessly stripping off the shirts they should have been proud to wear ... It was a disgusting scene ... '

These days Alex Ferguson or Arsène Wenger seem to defend their players for anything short of mass genocide, but in the 1970s things were different – and Brian Clough was *very* different. He said of his captain, 'Billy Bremner's behaviour was scandalous, producing one of the most notorious incidents in Wembley history. It was as if the players were offering grounds for all my criticism that they had resented so much.'

The nation was appalled. One spectator tried to have Bremner and Keegan charged with a breach of the peace, but a magistrate refused to issue a summons. The FA was less lenient, fining both players £500 and banning them for a staggering 11 matches. It would be October before Bremner played again, by which time the champions were struggling at the bottom of the league and Clough's ill-fated period at Leeds was over. For his part, Keegan made good use of his enforced holiday and got married.

Liverpool went on to win the game on penalties after Phil Boersma and Trevor Cherry made it 1-1, but by that point no one really cared.

WHEN CZECHS DON'T BOUNCE

Belgium v. Czechoslovakia
Olympic Football final, Antwerp, Belgium, 1920

Great Britain might have finally become excited about Olympic football in 2012, but the tournament has been running for over 100 years. In the early 20th century, pre-World Cup, the winners could truly claim to be World Champions and in both 1908 and 1912 the British amateurs had taken that title.

With no Olympics in war-torn 1916, the 1920 tournament in Antwerp was eagerly awaited. First-time entrants Czechoslovakia, scoring 15 and conceding just one, waltzed through to the final where they met hosts Belgium.

The match would remain the only international final to be abandoned – and naturally, it was officiated by an English referee and linesmen. The Czechs had already complained about the selection of John Lewis as referee, believing he bore a grudge against them after some harsh treatment during a match in Prague. Also, despite bearing the soubriquet of 'the Prince of Referees' in England, the 65-year-old Lewis's eyesight was failing and he struggled to do more than amble around.

Lewis did nothing to endear himself to the Czechs by awarding the hosts a dodgy penalty, a hotly disputed goal and failing to control some increasingly wild challenges. As half-time approached, Lewis reacted to Karel Steiner's hard challenge on Belgium's star player Robert Coppée by ordering the defender off the field. Czechoslovakia's captain Karel Pešek followed him in protest and pretty soon all the other players joined them.

With 40,000 fanatical fans going berserk and the pitch encircled by Belgian soldiers, the Czechs weren't inclined to return to the fray. Belgium were declared Olympic champions and the Eastern Europeans went home empty handed, the silver medal being decided by a hastily arranged play-off between Spain and the Netherlands.

▦ SENT OFF IN THE SHOOT-OUT

Botswana's captain and goalkeeper Modiri Marumo had put in a man-of-the-match performance to help his team to a 1-1 draw in a Castle Cup (the Southern African nations' competition) quarter-final against Malawi Flames in May 2003. With no extra time designated, the match went straight to penalties and all the clever money was on Marumo taking his Zebras through.

Unfortunately, Malawi started well, taking a 2-1 lead. As the Flames prepared for their third spot-kick, Marumo set about some mind-trickery time-wasting, irritating Mozambican referee Mateus Infante enough to receive a caution. Beaten by the penalty, the Zebras' keeper crossed over with his Malawian counterpart, Philip Nyasulu. As the opposing keeper tried to give him a conciliatory pat on the back of the head, Marumo reacted with a punch to the face. He became the only goalkeeper known to have received a red card during a penalty shoot-out.

After Botswana striker Tshepiso Molwantwa missed their third kick, defender Michael Mogaladi stepped up to take the keeper's place only for Malawi to take an unassailable 4-1 lead with a shot that he had little chance of stopping. Flames' captain Peter Mgangira received the man-of-the-match award and Maurmo was left to issue a most contrite apology, 'This unbecoming behaviour has not only embarrassed me but also the organisation that I work for, the Botswana Defence Force (BDF). I hope my apology will be recognised and I pledge my commitment in serving the nation.'

▦ NO SUCH THING AS A FRIENDLY

Portugal v. Angola
Friendly, Lisbon, 2001

Was this the night when 500 years of resentment came to the fore, when it was payback time for enslavement and vicious imperialism? Or did a few players just lose their heads?

The game was massive for Angola – a country whose national language is Portuguese, whose players mostly earned their living in Portugal, whose people fought a long war for independence and whose team were playing their first-ever match against their former colonial masters. For Portugal, it was a friendly, a chance for their golden generation – Figo, Couto, João Pinto et al – to prepare for the 2002 World Cup.

It all started so well for the underdogs. After only two minutes Mendonca found himself unmarked at the far post to put Angola one up. But 10 minutes later it started to unravel as Yamba Asha took out Portugal's Pauletta from behind. The striker retaliated by pushing Asha over, but only the Angolan was cautioned. Whatever the equivalent of an African's gander is, his was up and it wasn't coming down.

16 mins – Red Card No. 1: A fuming Asha, minutes after being booked, clatters into Petit: a second yellow and off.

25 mins – Red Card No. 2: Franklim lunges at João Pinto's knee as the forward goes into the area.

26 mins – Red Card No. 3: Estrela Wilson, a teammate of Franklim's at Portuguese club Belenenses, is shown two yellow cards inside 20 seconds for persistent dissent.

Half-time found Portugal 3-1 up with 45 minutes to play against eight-man Angola. They returned without Figo, Couto and Beto – a wise move as the Angolans hadn't finished yet. Knee-high challenges and scythes from behind went unpunished as the referee tried to save the game. Meanwhile, Angola coach Mario Calado made a flurry of substitutions, replacing virtually every one of his players left on the pitch.

63 mins – Red Card No. 4: Antonio Neto's wild kick takes a chunk out of João Tomas's thigh.

The remaining men soon conceded again to give the Portuguese a 5-1 lead, but with seven men now left, Angola needed just one more dismissal to get the match abandoned. On 67 minutes Angolan defender Helder Vicente suspiciously collapsed to the ground complaining of an injury. He was stretchered off, but Calado shrugged his shoulders; 'Oh dear! I've used all my subs,' he might

Angola's Helder Vicente is stretchered off with a slight tickle in the upper metatarsal. Well, you can't be too careful...

as well have said. Angola were now left with only six on-field players. It took just a quick check of his pocket book of FIFA rules before French referee Pascal Garibian declared the game abandoned.

In the aftermath Calado offered up one explanation, 'The referee unfortunately had a complex over an African team beating a Portuguese one.' Hmmm ...

TEN MEN WON THE LEAGUE – TRA-LA-LA-LA-LA!

Was this the greatest-ever display by 10 men? Certainly Celtic fans would tell you so, this match ranking second only to their European Cup triumph in 1967. Beating Rangers is always good, but to win the league in doing so is even sweeter – but the way they did it was sugar-coated butterscotch sweet ...

A winter-devastated fixture list had left the Old Firm derby at Parkhead on 21 May 1979 as Celtic's last game. The Bhoys had 46 points to their rivals' 43, but with another two easy matches to play the Blues were in pole position (these were two-points-for-a win days).

All the maths seemed a bit unnecessary when Rangers went in at half-time leading by Alex MacDonald's ninth-minute strike. Celtic, of course, would come out fighting and that's quite literally what fiery winger John Doyle did: aiming a kick at a prostrate MacDonald, whom he felt was time wasting. Referee Eddie Pringle had no option but to send the striker packing – back at Ibrox they were clearing a space in the trophy cabinet.

Back in the dressing room, Doyle sat with his head in his hands, but on the park Celtic, driven on by a frenzied crowd, surged forward in waves. They were finally rewarded on 67 minutes when Roy Aitken stabbed home an equaliser after a goalmouth scramble. Then just eight minutes later, the unthinkable happened as George McCluskey drove home after an Aitken shot was blocked. Miraculously the hooped men had done it – or had they?

An STV strike meant there was a TV blackout, but what happened next would live forever in the minds of those who were inside the ground that day. Inside two minutes the now delirious Jungle end of Parkhead was silenced again as Bobby Russell's shot through a crowded area found its way past Celtic's keeper Peter Latchford. Into the final 10 minutes, the weary 10 men in green sallied forth again. McCluskey sent a cross over, Rangers keeper Peter McCloy parried it straight on to Colin Jackson's head and watched in agony as it rebounded back into the net. It was to be Celtic's night – as a last-minute Murdo MacLeod goal sealed the match, the title and a legend.

While Celtic Park went berserk, one man was missing. A shell-shocked Johnny Doyle was still in the dressing room. 'I thought we had lost the championship because of me … If Celtic had lost, I had visions of collecting my boots and going.' It took a deputation from manager Billy McNeill to get him to emerge and join in the ecstatic celebrations.

▓ DISMISSED ON THEIR DEBUT

Whether you're a nervous 17-year-old or a seasoned international with a multi-million-pound price tag on your back, making your debut is a big affair. Some find it a doddle – Jimmy Greaves famously scored on his first outings for Chelsea, England, Spurs (a hat-trick), AC Milan and West Ham, and Wayne Rooney announced his Everton arrival with a superb strike against Arsenal and followed up with a three-goal debut for Man United against Fenerbahce.

On the other hand there's Jose Reyes, who marked his full Arsenal debut with a calamitous own goal against Middlesbrough and Burnley's Billy O'Rourke, who took his place in goal against QPR in 1979, and conceded seven. But, of course, we're here for the ultimate indignity – taking the big red one on your first time out. So, here are the top 10 debut dismissals …

Jason Crowe
Arsenal v. Birmingham, 1997
He was another of Wenger's wunderkinds – a production line that has produced the likes of Cesc Fabregas, Jermaine Pennant, and er, Arturo

Lupoli – taking the well-worn Carling Cup route. Except the usual lip-smacking headlines of young promise were not awaiting Jason; well, it's pretty hard to make an impression in just 33 seconds. That's how long extra-time substitute Crowe lasted on the pitch before a high tackle on Martin O'Connor saw Uriah Rennie sending the England Under-20 international packing.

Jonathan Woodgate
Real Madrid v. Athletic Bilbao, 2005

The *AS* newspaper headline 'Desastroso Debut De Woody' needed no translation. The injury-prone Woodgate had waited a year to make his Real Madrid debut after signing from Newcastle for £13.4 million. When he finally got his chance, he scored a spectacular first-half own goal and followed it up with a second yellow for a reckless challenge after 65 minutes. Woody would make only 14 appearances for Los Blancos before returning home to Middlesbrough. He was voted the worst signing of the century by Spanish newspaper *Marca*.

Joe Cole
Liverpool v. Arsenal, 2010

Joe Cole, a player that skipper Steven Gerrard rated as 'better than Lionel Messi', had gone to Liverpool to reignite a career that had stalled at Chelsea. Would the former England international finally fulfil his great promise? The Kop waited with bated breath as Liverpool kicked off their season against Arsenal, but Cole's only telling contribution came in first-half injury time as he hammered into the Gunners' new £10 million summer signing, Laurent Koscielny. Referee Mike Atkinson showed Cole the red card without hesitation and the former England international would have to wait another three games to begin his unimpressive Anfield stay. Not wanting to be outdone, fellow debutant Koscielny, despite being stretchered off after Cole's challenge, reappeared in the second half and by the end of the game had managed to earn a second yellow to join him in the Debut Dismissal Club.

Graeme Souness
Rangers v. Hibernian, 1986
Fresh from Sampdoria, Souness' arrival heralded a new era at Ibrox. Eager to make an impression, Rangers' new player-manager had picked up a yellow almost straight from the kick-off, but managed to last half an hour before launching himself at Hibs' George McCluskey – packing the ex-Celt off to casualty with lacerations to his knee. Souness walked and was handed a four-match ban – a sneak preview of his Ibrox days to come. To this day, however, Souness blames his then number two, Walter Smith, for his 37th-minute dismissal, telling the *Sun*, 'Walter told me to watch Billy Kirkwood as he'd try to catch me. I got the wrong player – but it was Walter's fault.'

Garry Flitcroft
Blackburn Rovers v. Everton, 1996
At the end of his debut, Premiership champions Blackburn Rovers had paid out precisely a million pounds a minute for the contribution of midfielder Garry Flitcroft. A £3 million signing from Manchester City, Flitcroft had seen out just three minutes when referee Jeff Winter waved the red card at him. Of course, it's just possible that Jeff had Flitcroft's interests at heart in consigning him to the trivia section – the combative midfielder had just elbowed Duncan Ferguson and 'Disorderly' would have had another 87 minutes to exact his revenge ...

Glenn Keeley
Everton v. Liverpool, 1982
Everton boss Howard Kendall took a gamble by giving on-loan Blackburn centre-back Keeley his first start in the high-octane Merseyside derby. The *Guardian* report noted that Kendall's 'faith could hardly have been more spectacularly betrayed'. After 37 minutes, Keeley tried swapping shirts with Dalglish a little early as King Kenny accelerated away. The Goodison faithful are a forgiving crowd but playing with 10 men for 53 minutes, four goals from Ian Rush and a record 5-0 defeat were hard to swallow. The burly defender would never play for the club again.

Ryan McGivern
Scotland v. Northern Ireland, 2008

Raising the stakes even further are those lads taking the Magenta Marker on their international debut. The fate of the young Lionel Messi is dealt with elsewhere (pages 109–110), but the less celebrated Ryan McGivern stepped up to the plate in a friendly at Hampden. Manchester City's 18-year-old full back managed to hang on to the famous green shirt (well, in this case white with green pinstripes) for nearly an hour before picking up his second yellow for a clumsy challenge on Scott Brown. Like Messi, Ryan thankfully saw his international career continue despite the setback.

Tony Cottee
Liverpool v. West Ham, 1994

As a 17-year-old, the West Ham fox-in-the-box had marked his debut with a poacher's goal against Spurs and, when a £2.2 million deal took him to Everton in 1988, he kicked off his career as a Toffee with a goal in 34 seconds and a subsequent hat-trick against Newcastle. So, much was expected when Tony returned to West Ham and prepared for his second Hammers debut, at Anfield. But, his luck had run out – as, rather than his name on the score sheet, it was written on the back of a red card.

Dennis Wise
Millwall v. Sheffield United, 2003

'There was a sense that what we were watching wasn't really a football match, but the answer to a future pub quiz question,' wrote Mark Hodgkinson in the *Daily Telegraph*. Dennis the Menace picked up 13 red cards in his career but saved the best for last. In his first game as player-manager of Millwall in 2003, Dennis watched from the dugout as his team were coasting to a 2-0 victory over Sheffield United. Keen to stretch his legs for five minutes, Dennis brought himself on. For all of two minutes, The Den saw its new hero's customary cheeky chappy/snarling tiger act. Then he was back in the dugout – having seen red after a two-footed lunge on Chris Armstrong.

His 12 reds had earned Dennis the right to pick his victim before coming on as sub.

WHAT HAPPENED NEXT?

→ • • • • • • • • • • • • • • •

Taking a lead from the mildly amusing round of *A Question of Sport*, this chapter takes the red card as the starting point and waits for the consequences, hilarious or otherwise. You might think the game has reached boiling point when the dreaded red comes out, but so often this is just the cue for things to really kick off: players flipping out, teams walking off, refs losing the plot and depleted sides being inspired to fight their way back ...

A FUNNY THING HAPPENED ON THE WAY TO THE TOUCHLINE

The ref's doing that wheels-on-the-bus movement with his hands and the fourth official has finally got a piece of the action by holding up his digital numbers. That's it, your time's up. No more chances to impress the boss or help your team. Or are there?

You still have the walk across the pitch – according to the rules, in a straight line – in which to influence events. You can still have a motivational word with a teammate, wind up an opponent or waste a little time. It was the latter that was on the mind of Rui Costa as Portugal were holding out for a 1-1 draw in a 1998 World Cup qualifier against Germany in Berlin.

As 'O Maestro', one of the greatest players of his generation, reached spitting distance of the touchline, the irate ref caught up with him and showed him a second yellow. He told Fifa.com, 'My substitution only took 22 seconds but the referee showed me a red card ... it was the only time I've ever been sent off in my entire footballing career.' Portugal successfully saw out the draw, but it wasn't enough to see them through to the finals in France.

Stranger still was the incident that led to Ghanaian international Samuel Inkoom seeing red in Ukraine. Inkoom's Dnipro were two goals up against Karpaty Lviv in a Ukrainian Premier League match when his boss Juande Ramos called for his substitution in the 62nd minute. The defender made a beeline for the bench without dallying, but removed his shirt before crossing the touchline. As the ever-useful fourth official grabbed the bemused Inkoom's attention, he looked back to see referee Derevinsky (possibly Russian for 'jobsworth') brandishing a second yellow and the fateful red.

AND THAT'S FOR ONE YOU DID EARLIER

In all the fuss surrounding Palestine's first-ever World Cup match, a bizarre sending-off crept under the radar. Hong Kong were their hosts in the qualifier for the 2000 World Cup finals, a tight match which was balanced at 1-1 as the game's final minutes drew near.

A bad tackle by Hong Kong's English-born John Moore led to South Korean ref Han Byung-hwa booking the former Sunderland and Hull City player. But while the ref was scribbling in his notebook, his Yemeni assistant on the line had a word. Moore had been involved in an altercation 10 minutes earlier that the lino thought had been worthy of a yellow too. Without further thought, the ref produced a second yellow and then a red.

Retrospective action – it might just catch on!

MAINE ROAD REFUSENIKS

With City's Arab-inspired resurgence, the Manchester derby is once again getting frisky, but it'll take some doing to match the events of 1974 at City's Maine Road home when all 22 men were ordered off the park.

Many remember the corresponding tie at Old Trafford that season – the final league match that saw Denis Law help his former club towards relegation with a nifty backheel. Fewer will recall the sparky encounter earlier in the season, but the events are still clear in United's Lou Macari's mind. He told the *Guardian* in November 2000, 'I hit the deck after Mike Doyle, surprise, surprise, chopped me down ... I bounced straight back up again and threw the ball in his direction. It hit him on the shoulder or the side of his ear.' Doyle, always keen to take up arms against a Red, hit back – and the whistle went.

They expected a booking, but were shocked to see Clive 'The Book' Thomas sending both of them for a proverbial early one. Macari and Doyle did walk ... away – as if nothing had happened. For all his pointing Thomas couldn't persuade them to leave the field. So the ref, never one to hide from controversy, picked up the ball and took both teams off the field.

As the crowd waited in confusion, Thomas gave the teams a couple of minutes thinking time before visiting both dressing rooms in the company of two burly police officers. He told both teams that he expected them to return to the field immediately, paused, pointed at the offending players and said – without them. Sure enough, back they came for a dull 0-0 draw. Good old Clive, so often providing the brightest moment of a match.

▦ LOOKING AFTER NUMBER ONE

Goalies' position of last resort gives them a special place in the red card annals – especially when there's no one gloved-up on the subs' bench. It's a rare sight these days, but it takes you back to *Saint and Greavsie*, muddy quagmires at the Baseball Ground and Ipswich as title challengers, when the dismissal of the man in green (as goalies always were then) would take the game in a hilarious, unexpected direction.

An outfield player – often, as it seemed to be chosen at random, the best or shortest player in the team – would swap shirts with the departing No. 1 and put on his gloves. He'd then stand in the goal, which suddenly appeared twice as big, looking like a kid wearing his big brother's hand-me-downs, while opponents attempted to shoot from any distance and angle. The big question now was: would he be a hero or a clown?

Sir Matt Busby once claimed that George Best was not only the best striker, midfielder and defender at Manchester United, but he was also the best goalkeeper. He never got a chance, but some other famous names did …

Niall Quinn
Manchester City v. Derby County, 1991
Having already put City ahead, the 6-foot-4-inch Irishman squeezed into Tony Coton's shirt after the keeper had been ordered off for a professional foul. Like a strip from *Roy of the Rovers*, the acrobatic stand-in goalie then plunged full length to his left to keep out Dean Saunders' penalty. A former Gaelic football player, Quinn looked happier than most in front of the net – so much so that the Republic of Ireland named him as third-choice keeper at Italia 90, even though he was their first-choice striker.

Robbie Savage
Derby County v. Reading, 2011

The ballroom dancer, radio celebrity and one time 'hardman with a bouffant' still dines out on the story of his magnificent goalkeeping performance. After replacement keeper Saul Deeney was sent off for a professional foul just before half-time, Robbie 'Southall' Savage faced down Shane Long's sky-high penalty before performing heroics between the sticks, including an acrobatic tip over the bar from a free-kick. He still let two in, though, as the Rams went down 4-1. 'It is the most boring position in the world to be fair, isn't it?' Savage said afterwards. 'It is horrendous.'

Vinnie Jones
Newcastle United v. Wimbledon, 1995

It was the era of Ferdinand, Ginola and Beardsley, and the season Newcastle blew a 12-point title lead. Jones donned the gloves after Paul Heald got sent off for two bookings and, although Newcastle won 6-1, Hollywood Vinnie did himself proud with an incredible double save, diving full length to parry David Ginola's low shot from outside the box, then recovering to push Keith Gillespie's follow-up on to the post. The final whistle saw Jones receive a standing ovation from the Geordie faithful.

Rio Ferdinand
Manchester United v. Portsmouth, 2008

Rio can turn his hands to most things – rapping, homemade porn, tweeting – so naturally he's an accomplished glovesman. When Tomasz Kuszczak brought down Milan Baros at Old Trafford in an FA Cup quarter-final, England's future skipper pulled on the No. 1 shirt and tried to save the resultant spot-kick and United's day. He valiantly flung himself the right way and nearly got a hand to it, but Sulley Muntari's penalty flew past him for the only goal of the game. Rio acquitted himself well for the remaining 12 minutes of the match, but United's hopes of a second treble were blown.

▓ MAN TO MANKINI MARKING

How does Borat, comedian Sacha Baron Cohen's character from an obscure former Soviet republic, make it into a football book? A full four years after the mockumentary film *Cultural Learnings of America for Make Benefit Glorious Nation of Kazakhstan*, Alan Young, a Havant and Waterlooville fan, decided to pay homage to Borat by running back and forth on the pitch dressed only in a bright green 'mankini' and white socks. Unfortunately his team were involved in a Blue Square Bet South match against Dorchester Town at the time …

Conceding an equaliser had infuriated Dorchester Town's 39-year-old player-manager Ashley Vickers and the sight of a near naked bloke in a silly wig evading hapless stewards didn't lighten his mood.

Dorchester Town's new away strip broke every rule in FIFA's kit regulations.

Taking the situation in hand, he not only caught the pitch-invader but drove him rugby-forward style a full five yards before pulling him to the ground. Young later told the BBC, 'It was only a bit of a joke, we all agreed at my local pub on Sunday I'd do it as a bet ... The security there were too slow, but Vickers caught me quite well. He should be a rugby player.'

Dusting himself down, Vickers looked up modestly to accept the referee's thanks only to find himself staring at the red square. Even the Havant players were amazed and pleaded his case – their chairman even offering to take a man off to even things up. Vickers himself told the *Dorset Echo*, 'I'm dumbfounded and speechless ... My only thought was to get hold of him so we could get on with the game. I managed to grab him and bring him to the ground and the funny thing was the stewards actually thanked me for it.'

PUT YOUR PANTS ON AND COME BACK OUT TO BE DISCIPLINED

It was a tense 2008 Steel City derby. Mike Dean had already dished out a red to United's Matthew Kilgallon for a high challenge, but the game could still go either way. It was the kind of match every player wants to play in, but for Wednesday's Jermaine Johnson it was about to come to an end. After 67 minutes manager Brian Laws was replacing the winger, who had been a livewire all day.

Johnson was furious. He left the field but, before storming down the tunnel, he angrily kicked a plastic bottle into the crowd and pushed away a sympathetic Wednesday coach. So far, so what? It was what happened next which entered the bizarre books ...

After being alerted to the bottle incident by his assistant, Dean called a halt to the game. Four minutes elapsed as the Jamaica winger – already stripped down to his vest – was brought back from the changing room to the touchline. There, Dean issued him with a yellow card and, since he had already been cautioned, he was then presented with a red.

As he had left the field before the incident, Wednesday were allowed to continue with 11 men against the Blades' 10 and just eight minutes later Steve Watson's goal won the match for the Owls.

WHEN THE ERIC HIT THE FAN

By the 1990s, we'd grown tired of fans attacking fans and bored of players assaulting fellow professionals – where could the ill-discipline junkie turn now for kicks? Enter the King – Eric Cantona – with one of the great flashpoints of football history.

Wednesday 25 January 1995 was a cold night at Selhurst Park as high-flying visitors Manchester United took on strugglers Crystal Palace. The home side's player of the year, Richard Shaw, had practically marked the Gallic genius out of the game in the first half. He'd got away with a number of niggly kicks and still hadn't seen a yellow.

Back after the break, frustrated and disappointed, Cantona rose with Shaw to contest a high ball. As they descended, the Frenchman aimed a crafty kick at his rival and out came referee Alan Wilkie's red card. Cantona was dismissed for the fifth time in 16 months. Eric looked upset, but calm as he began to trudge off the field. He turned down his trademark raised collar and – as his manager Ferguson studiously looked the other way – headed along the touchline to the dressing room. The sending off was inconvenient, but what followed was almost apocalyptic.

Matthew Simmons was only one of thousands of Palace fans screaming abuse at the United player, but rushing down 10 rows of seats to make sure his voice was heard, he clearly caught Eric's attention. A qualified referee, perhaps Simmons was riled by Cantona's flagrant infringement of the misconduct rules, or possibly he just didn't like foreigners. Either way, he had lit King Eric's fuse.

Cantona leapt at the fan feet first, delivering a well-aimed boot in the face. He managed to follow up with a couple of punches before being led away by United keeper Peter Schmeichel and kit man

Norman Davies. United midfielder Paul Ince arrived just late enough on the scene to deliver his fabulous line, 'Come on, we'll take you all on!'

The whole incident had lasted under 90 seconds and yet would fill papers and news bulletins for days. FA chief executive Graham Kelly sanctimoniously called the attack 'a stain on our game' and banned Cantona for nine months. The courts then gave him to a two-week

Eric would practise his back post volleys whenever he had a chance.

prison sentence (downgraded to 120 hours of community service on appeal).

Perhaps worst of all, the incident led to the player uttering his famous and unintelligible sardine and trawler quote, which somehow transformed him from mercurial player with a filthy temper into a deep thinker with a tortured existential soul – and prepared him nicely for a post-football life in deep French films in which nothing much happens ...

THE COMEBACK FROM HELL

Euro 2000, in Belgium and the Netherlands, found Slovenia playing in their first-ever major international competition – not bad for a country that had existed for less than 10 years. Understandably, anticipation was high in the Balkan state – especially as they were playing Yugoslavia, the country that they had been part of for most of the 20th century, in their opening game.

The Yugoslavians were past their best, but still listed the likes of Stankovic, Kovacevic and Mihajlovic in their number; while the Slovenians, with Zlatko Zahovic their only star, were 150-1 rank-outsiders at the start of the tournament.

Back home in Slovenia supporters were delighted as their team went in at half-time leading by Zahovic's diving header; elated to go two-up after 53 minutes; and on cloud nine when their hero notched his second before the hour was up. 'Only a natural disaster can save Yugoslavia now,' cried the Slovenian commentator. There were no disasters, just the red mist of Sinisa Mihajlovic, the mad 'Bomber'. Two bookings in as many minutes saw the Yugoslavians down to 10 men. Surely the match was won now?

Anyone remember Savo Milosevic, the unimpressive 1990s striker nicknamed 'Miss-a-lot-evic' by Aston Villa fans? For it was he who led an amazing comeback as the 10-strong Yugoslavians pulled back all three goals in six minutes. Savo tapped home two simple goals either side of a Drulovic angled drive to complete what captain Dragan Stojkovic would call the 'Comeback from Hell'.

▦ THAT'S PANTS THAT IS ...

Question: When did FIFA turn refs into *Viz*-styled Knicker Inspectors? Answer: In 2011 when they amended Rule 4 to oblige officials to ensure undergarments are of the same colour as the shorts themselves. This jobsworthy dirty laundry would be aired when Newport County took on Bath City in a FA Youth Cup tie at their Spytty Park ground.

Bath City's Under-18 team looked neatly turned out in their away strip of red shirts with white trim and red shorts. But something under the shorts was amiss – and for eagle-eyed referee Darren Adie, one glance up an outstretched leg was enough to spot a flagrant breach of the FA regulation.

After 20 or so minutes, while a City player was receiving treatment from the trainer, the referee caught a telltale glimpse of white cycling shorts underneath his team issue shorts. He directed the player to leave the field to change and, for good measure, gave the same order to a teammate who he had identified as sporting similarly offensive boxer shorts.

Perhaps this story might have ended with a few giggles from the massed 149 spectators as the players went commando pitchside had not County scored while Bath were down to nine men. All hell broke loose, resulting in one of the offending players, City boss Clark and a substitute all seeing red. Three others, including the keeper, later followed them to the dressing room and unsurprisingly County strolled to a 6-0 victory.

After the match, as the referee locked himself inside his dressing room, livid City chairman Manda Rigby told the *Bath Chronicle* (to an accompaniment of schoolboy tittering), 'It was farcical – I have never seen anything like it before.'

▦ SECONDS OUT ... ROUND TWO

Lee and Hunter

Derby County v. Leeds United, 1975

There were some great fights in the 1970s, Ali v. Frazier, Duran v. Leonard, but of them all Lee v. Hunter took some beating. This was back in the days when men were men and forwards were nervous. Few inspired more nerves than Norman 'bites yer legs' Hunter, but equally rare were those as nerveless as the pit-bull-framed Franny Lee. On a chilly day at the Baseball Ground in November 1975, the immovable object met the irresistible force ...

The previous season English champions Derby had knocked Leeds off their perch. Old foes Brian Clough and Don Revie had now been replaced by Dave Mackay and Jimmy Armfield, so many thought their rivalry would have dissipated. Lee and Hunter were about to prove them wrong.

With the scores level at 1-1, Lee took one of his famous (he wasn't called Lee Won Pen for nothing) tumbles in the penalty area. To Hunter's dismay, referee Derek Nippard bought it hook, line and sinker and awarded Derby a spot-kick. As Charlie George converted the penalty, Lee turned to Hunter and gave him the cheekiest of winks.

Norm wasn't one to brood for long and, at the next opportunity after Lee had just taken a shot, he clipped him from behind. Lee jumped up to confront the man who had been his room-mate at Mexico 70, but Hunter wasn't into the handbags and empty gestures. His left hook connected with Lee's mouth with enough force to split his lip. Players from both teams joined in the traditional pushing and shoving and by the time Nippard had calmed everyone down it became apparent that both combatants had been dismissed.

The ref was still filling their names in his little book when Paul Reaney tugged at his arm to draw attention to events developing at the side of the pitch. Unable to get as far as the touchline without raising unfinished business, Lee had gone at the bigger man with a flurry of punches. Hunter, with a longer reach was picking his shots, but lost his balance as he backed off. Teammates rushed to 'separate' the brawlers – Archie Gemmill, Billy Bremner and others ensuring a few more blows were delivered before the ref arrived.

The whole thing was shown in detail on *Match of the Day* where John Motson described how 'a side to football we really do not want to see has unfortunately reared its ugly head' – thousands disagreed, as the scrap was re-enacted in playgrounds across the country.

Hunter had borne a grudge ever since his roommate squeezed his toothpaste from the middle ...

YOU'RE A RECORD BREAKER!

→ • • • • • • • • • • • •

'Dedication's what you need if you want to be a record breaker, yeah.' So sang Roy Castle in the theme tune from 1970s BBC TV show *Record Breakers*. When it comes to red cards he was partly right: you do need dedication, but some other attributes help. Like a powder-keg temper, an ability to hype yourself into orbit, a target-seeking flying elbow and a jobsworth official who has got out of bed the wrong side …

▦ GEORGE BEST GETS FIRST EVER RED CARD IN ENGLAND – ALMOST

In 1976, at the same time that red and yellow cards were introduced to English football, George Best was attempting to get his football career back on the rails. Three years after his last, sad turnouts for Manchester United, the 28-year-old Best joined Bobby Moore and Rodney Marsh at second division Fulham's veteran Galacticos.

Best, who had spent the summer in the North American Soccer League with Los Angeles Aztecs, had got off to a flier for the Cottagers scoring three times in their first five games. However, on 2 October, down at Southampton's Dell, he protested against a free kick using foul and abusive language to referee Lester Shapter (known as the 'Whistling Albino'). Shapter raised the new-fangled red card and Best was off. Before that Saturday, no one in the Football League had participated in this particular piece of football theatre.

So was Best the first player to receive the red card? Unfortunately not. David Wagstaffe, in his time a fine winger at Wolves, was also playing out his career. On for Blackburn Rovers against Orient, he had managed to see red a few minutes ahead of the alcohol-fuelled, Northern Irish genius ... So nearly a great red card story!

▦ MOST RED CARDS IN ONE GAME

19: In 2009 the Europeans went for the record as Recreativo Linense took on Saladillo de Algeciras in a Spanish regional league first division match. Recreativo were 1-0 up when referee Jose Manuel Barro Escandón red-carded one of their number in the 54th minute. A subsequent mass fight broke out, which was escalated by the participation of several members of the crowd. Escandón abandoned the match and took shelter in his changing room, emerging much later to show red cards to anyone he could remember being involved. Raising the card nine times in each dressing room, he managed to get the count to 19 ... close but no cigar.

20: In a Paraguayan league match between between Sportivo Ameliano and General Caballero in 1993, the ref's decision to dismiss two Sportivo players led to a 10-minute onfield dust-up. The official proceeded to show his red card to an at that time unprecedented 18 more players. The match, unsurprisingly, was abandoned. Could do better.

But in the number one spot is 36: And this is going to take some beating ... Buenos Aires teams Club Atlético Claypole and Victoriano Arenas play in the fifth tier of Argentine football. Imagine Kidderminster against Forest Green. As their 2011 tussle descended into a running riot, referee Damian Rubino issued 36 red cards, including all 22 players, both teams' substitutes, some of the technical staff and maybe even a local hot dog vendor.

▦ A LITTLE BIT OF AFTERS

Not one red card was shown in 90 minutes or the seven more minutes of added time, but Bradford City and Crawley Town still managed to equal the English league record for red cards in March 2012.

Kick-off in this match took place just seconds after the final whistle. Players seem to have come together to shake hands, but at that point Bradford's patience finally snapped (Crawley had collected six bookings to their hosts' none) and a running brawl erupted from nowhere.

Safely ensconced in their dressing rooms after the fracas, the teams received a visit from referee Ian Williamson, who'd noted who'd larruped whom, and had come to deliver the red cards in person – three to Bradford and two for the visitors.

THE MERSEY RUNS RED

Liverpool against Everton brings forth pictures of families sporting blue and red sitting together, opposing fans spoiling each other with their marvellous sense of humour and two teams bound in respect, preferring to reserve their ire for the folk down the East Lancs Road ...Twaddle!

The *Daily Telegraph* has referred to the Merseyside derby as, 'the most ill-disciplined and explosive fixture in the Premier League,' and they have the stats to back it up. It is, by some distance the most red-card scarred match in the fixture list with 21 red cards issued in as many years (compare that to the Manchester derby that has seen just five red cards in the Premier League era or the North London derby's seven).

Everton are 12-9 up on the tally (do they care more?) with the distinction of having finished the match with nine men on four occasions. Steven Gerrard and Phil Neville have the honour of making the list twice. Stevie G's second saw him walk off sporting the number 08 in honour of Liverpool being the City of Culture that year, while Phil's diving injury-time save in 2007 would have salvaged a draw for Everton – if Dirk Kuyt hadn't converted the penalty.

THREE CARDS TO THE WINDASS

Dean Windass, a cult hero at Hull City and Bradford City, notched up a massive nine red cards in his career – a fair haul for a striker. But to be fair, like buses, three arrived at once as his Aberdeen side played Dundee United in a league fixture in 1997.

Windass – who famously grabbed the crown jewels of Cheltenham Town's John Finnigan on FIFA's Fair Play Day – was well up for a match that Aberdeen had to win to save manager Roy Aitken's job. Windass had already caught the referee's eye after being booked for a reckless challenge in the opening minute and it took him little more than 20 minutes of hyped-up charging around to take the high road to the dressing room.

After producing the red card, referee Stuart Dougal had the full list of all the cuss words Deano had picked up on his long career blasted down his ears at full volume. With steam hissing from his head, Windass finally stomped off. He got as far as the corner flag and thought of one final protest. Deano ripped out the flag and threw it to the ground. Yes, that'll show him I'm upset, he probably thought.

After Aberdeen had succumbed to a 5-0 defeat (they were already 3-0 down when Deano walked), Dougal visited Windass and Aitken. He explained how the striker had actually received three red cards: one for his two yellows, one for dissent and a third for abuse of field furniture. It resulted in a record 22 points in one game (coincidentally, one for every minute he'd played), an eight-week ban and a fine of a month's wages.

But Deano was still three short of the record ...

Having run out of expletives, Deano was reduced to schoolyard insults as he attempted to improve on three reds.

▦ HIT FOR SIX

In November 2009 Hawick United's Paul Cooper was shown six (6! SIX, VI! – as the teleprinter might add) red cards in the same match – and that was a record.

Hawick had met Pencaitland in the Border Amateur League when the striker received his second yellow for dissent. On getting the obligatory red, Paul, nicknamed 'Santa', went nuclear. Before he left the pitch he told referee Andy Lyon where he could shove his card – in a number of different ways. Five red cards later, he finally took his leave. He was given a two-year ban, a career-ending suspension for a 39-year-old. 'I love football but I'll now have to find something else to do on a Saturday,' he told the BBC.

▦ JAM TARTS GET BURNT AT IBROX

'It's always difficult when you're playing against seven men,' was one cliché Walter Smith didn't bother stooping to when Hearts went into meltdown in 1996. After a Gazza-inspired Rangers ran the Edinburgh team ragged in the first half, a full complement of maroon shirts had taken to the Ibrox dressing room just 1-0 down. But, with four already in referee Jerry Evans' book they would, as the commentators say, be walking a tightrope in the second half.

And, it wasn't too long before they began to plunge. Just three minutes after the restart, cult hero Pasquale Bruno – carrying a caution and trying to pretend his nickname wasn't 'The Animal' – tripped Gordon Durie and was sent on his way. A Gascoigne goal settled the affair soon after, but Hearts felt the Glasgow faithful needed a little more to warm them than a meagre Scotch Pie. They settled for an eight-minute performance of a little known Scottish farce called 'Get Tae F***'.

On the hour, David Weir got physical with Durie and, after trying unsuccessfully to engage three other Rangers players, walked off. Three minutes later, a frustrated Neil Pointon kicked a post, did an angry pointing-and-shouting-at-the-linesman routine and entered the book for a second time. Five whole minutes passed before the lino decided a walk-on part wasn't enough. He called the ref over and off went Paul Ritchie under whatever rule 'looking at me in a funny way' comes.

Now, one more red would mean the whole game would be abandoned. With Hearts chief executive Chris Robinson threatening to take the rest of the team off, Richard Gough calmed things down. He probably didn't say, 'Let Jukebox [Durie] have another goal and we'll call it a day,' but he might as well have done.

▦ 'VIOLENCE OF THE TONGUE'

While debate in Europe raged over Geoff Hurst's did-it-didn't-it goal in the 1966 World Cup final, down in South America they still hadn't got over the quarter-finals. Their suspicions that foul play had been used to get the host nation to the final were fuelled by the famous dismissal of Argentina's skipper and talisman, Antonio Rattin.

Rattin was the ultimate enforcer, a tall uncompromising midfielder who hustled and physically intimidated his opponents, but also knew what to do with the ball. Tactically clever and a superb organiser, he was also a brilliant captain – a man the Albiceleste could ill-afford to lose in such a crucial game.

Many, presumably including German referee, Rudolf Kreitlein, were expecting Argentina, who had been officially warned about their brutal play by FIFA, to come out kicking at Wembley. In the event, their approach was more niggly than physical, but it was Rattin's constant sniping at Kreitlein that most irked the referee. By the 35th minute, the ref had obviously had enough. He had already booked Rattin, so after one incandescent complaint too many he sent the Argentina captain packing – officially for 'violence of the tongue' although he later added something about 'I didn't like the way he looked at me!'

Rattin had no intention of walking. It took eight minutes to get him off the pitch. Ken Aston, official supervisor of referees, came on but failed to persuade him and the help of a translator was enlisted. Eventually he trudged off, but then hung around the sidelines, sitting (with his muddy boots) on the Queen's red carpet before being ushered towards the dressing room. But still Rattin wasn't finished and in a not-altogether-understandable symbolic gesture, he grabbed and deliberately crumpled the England pennant attached to the corner flag. Ooooh! Get you!

Kreitlein fails to find 'looking at me in a funny way' in his pocket rule book, but sends the Argentinian off anyway.

Without their inspirational skipper Argentina were a lesser force, although after 90 minutes only a single Hurst header separated the teams. While Alf Ramsey intervened in the shirt swapping and, unfairly, raged about 'animals', England celebrated reaching the World Cup semi-final for the first ever time.

Thousands of miles away another paragraph was being written in a conspiracy theory that had already taken shape. How could Kreitlein object to Rattin's language when he knew no Spanish and Rattin no German? Ignoring the obvious constant dissent, South American football fans added this to a list of grievances: the lack of protection Pelé had received, decisions given by the English ref against Uruguay, something about a dodgy official draw and, possibly, something about a grassy knoll – and came to the conclusion that South America had been cheated.

▦ RED CARD RECORDS

Most Premier League red cards
8: Richard Dunne, Duncan Ferguson, Patrick Vieira
7: Vinnie Jones, Roy Keane, Franck Queudrue, Alan Smith
6: Eric Cantona, Lee Cattermole, John Hartson

Sent off for most Premier League clubs
5: Carlton Palmer – Leeds United, Sheffield Wednesday, Southampton, Coventry City and Nottingham Forest

Most red cards in a Premier League season
75: in 2005-06

Most red cards in a Premier League season (by club)
9: Sunderland in 2009-10 and QPR in 2011-12

Fewest red cards in a Premier League season
33: in 1993-94

Most red cards in a Premier League match

3: Manchester City v. Tottenham Hotspur, November 2008
Portsmouth v. Sunderland, February 2010

Premier League all-time red card totals (by team)

75: Blackburn Rovers
71: Everton
64: Arsenal
61: Chelsea
59: West Ham United
58: Newcastle United
53: Manchester City
52: Tottenham Hotspur
51: Manchester United
45: Liverpool
44: Aston Villa, Middlesbrough, Sunderland
43: Bolton Wanderers
35: Southampton
31: Fulham
28: Leicester City, Wimbledon
27: Leeds United
26: Birmingham City, Wigan Athletic
23: Coventry City
21: Charlton Athletic
20: Portsmouth, Queens Park Rangers, Sheffield Wednesday, West Bromwich Albion
16: Derby County
14: Stoke City
12: Wolverhampton Wanderers

Most Football League red cards

13: Roy McDonough, Steve Walsh
12: Mark Dennis:

Most red cards in a Football League match

5: Chesterfield v. Plymouth Argyle, League Division Two, February 1997 (see pages 95–6)

Bristol Rovers v. Wigan Athletic, League Division Two, December 1997
Exeter City v. Cambridge United, League Division Three, November 2002
Bradford City v. Crawley Town, League Division Two, March 2012

Most red cards in a British professional career
21: Willie Johnstone, Roy McDonough

Fastest red cards
World (top tier): 10 seconds
Giuseppe Lorenzo, Bologna v. Parma, Serie A, Italy, December 1990
International football: 35 seconds
Rashed Al Hooti, Bahrain v. Iran, Asian Cup qualifier, October 2011
England (top tier): 85 seconds
Liam O'Brien, Manchester United v. Southampton, January 1987
Premier League: 72 seconds
Tim Flowers, Blackburn Rovers v. Leeds United, February 1995
Football League: 13 seconds
Kevin Pressman, Sheffield Wednesday v. Wolverhampton Wanderers, August 2000.
Non-League: 3 seconds
David Pratt, Chippenham Town v. Bashley, Southern League Premier Division, January 2009

'Hit 'em hard and hit 'em early' used to be the mantra. But all you need is a ref up for making a name for himself and you're back in the dressing room before the subs have even had a chance to rifle through your trouser pockets. This was the fate of Manchester United's Liam O'Brien, dismissed after 85 seconds in the first tackle of the game against Southampton in 1987. But Chippenham Town's David Pratt didn't want to bother with such niceties as tackles. Bashley's kick-off drew a two-footed lunge from the striker. He was off in just three seconds. As for Bologna's Lorenzo, he was a little too hyped-up and went for a spot of fisticuffs straight from the off.

Goalkeepers have been in the line of fire ever since FIFA introduced the 'preventing a goalscoring opportunity' clause in 1990. Crewe keeper Mark Smith set a record for the fastest ever red card in Football League history when he was dismissed for a professional foul against Darlington in March 1994, but records are there to be broken. Tim Flowers took out Leeds' Brian Deane (breaking his own toe in the process) to get his red – while Kevin Pressman knocked almost a minute off that by handling outside the area in the first attacking move of the match. The Sheffield Wednesday keeper claimed the ball had hit his chest, but stayed in the record books as the FA's right of appeal is limited to mistaken identity, violent conduct and serious foul play.

Pride of place goes to Cross Farm Park Celtic striker Lee Todd. Todd had his back to the referee as his team prepared to kick off in a Sunday league game against Taunton East Reach Wanderers in October 2000. As the ref blew to start the match, Todd turned to him and remarked, 'F*** me, that was loud!' Lee was shown the red card with just *two* seconds on the clock.

Sent off in consecutive matches against the same team

Nemanja Vidic: in October 2009 the Serb was sent off for the third successive time in a Manchester United v. Liverpool match.

Fastest red card for a substitute on the field of play

0 seconds: Walter Boyd, Swansea City v. Darlington, March 2000
Keith Gillespie, Sheffield United v. Reading, January 2007

You've done a few stretches, a couple of sprints up the touchline and shouted some abuse at the opposition winger. Now it's time to get on and do some damage ... if you can actually make it that far.

Young Gunner Jason Crowe and Lionel Messi have been mentioned elsewhere in this book, but they all put in a full shift compared to Macclesfield's Vinny Mukendi, who had been playing for a full seven seconds before he went for using his elbow in an aerial challenge against Burton Albion. Still, at least he had time to work up a bead of sweat, which is more than the record holders: Jamaican international Walter Boyd and former 'next Ryan Giggs' Keith Gillespie. Both were

The legendary Scouse wit. Even Vidic had to laugh.

sent off in kerfuffles that erupted before play had restarted, so technically had not played a single second.

While we're here, there are a couple of other players that have earned a mention. In 1999, Aberdeen's Nigel Pepper was sent off just six minutes after coming on as a sub against Celtic. Having served his suspension, he was desperate to get off the bench in their game against Dundee United. This time he lasted 15 seconds. Then there's Auxerre defender Jean-Pascal Mignot who managed to get two yellows for dissent in a Champions League tie against Ajax – and hadn't even left the bench.

First ever red card
David Wagstaffe: Blackburn Rovers v. Leyton Orient, October 1976

Youngest player to receive red card in Premier League
Wayne Rooney: Everton v. Birmingham City, December 2002

Rooney lasted 16 minutes after coming on as a 65th-minute substitute at St Andrews before his two-footed lunge on Steve Vickers – the defender needing eight stitches. The Roonster was 17 years and 63 days old.

Goalkeeper with most red cards in the Premier League
Jussi Jaaskelainen (Bolton Wanderers): 4

On 5 January 2008, Dagenham and Redbridge's Tony Roberts became the first goalkeeper to be sent off in the FA Cup in the opposition's area after a fracas with Southend's Peter Clarke.

On 16 October 1993, Colchester United became the first league club to have two goalkeepers sent off in one match. During their game against Hereford United, John Keeley and Nathan Munson were both dismissed for professional fouls as the Us collapsed to a 5-0 defeat at Hereford's Edgar Street.

Wembley Stadium – role of dis-honour

First sending off at original Wembley Stadium

Antonio Rattin, Argentina v. England, World Cup quarter-finals, July 1966 (see pages 77–9)

First club players to be sent off at original Wembley Stadium

Kevin Keegan (Liverpool) and Billy Bremner (Leeds United), Charity Shield, August 1974 (see pages 46–8)

Last club player to receive red card at original Wembley Stadium

Justin Edinburgh, Tottenham Hotspur v. Leicester City, League Cup final, March 1999

First (and only) England player to receive red card at original Wembley Stadium

Paul Scholes v. Sweden, June 1999 (see pages 30–1)

First player to receive red card at new Wembley

Matthew Gill, Exeter City v. Morecambe, Conference National Play-off, May 2007

First league player to receive red card at new Wembley

Marc Tierney, Shrewsbury v. Bristol Rovers, League Two Play-off, May 2007

WHO'S THE ****ER IN THE BLACK?

→ • • • • • • • • • • • • •

There's the defender who elbows the tricky winger in the face, the studs-up midfielder's knee-high challenge or the cheating, diving centre-forward – but who's the real villain? Yes, it's the probation officer, history teacher, traffic warden who's had a humour-bypass and fancies himself as a cross between Mussolini and Barnum as soon as he tucks that red card in his pocket.

OK, it's a thankless task, they're only human (probably) and without them the game – and this book – is nothing, but no one *asked* them to do it ...

WHEN MEN WERE MEN

It's often said that you needed to do something pretty awful to get sent off in olden days' black and white football. But was that always the case? The story of Billy Elliott (nope, not that one), the Burnley and England left winger of the 1940s, suggests otherwise.

Billy was a hard case and not averse to getting his retaliation in first on opposing full backs. But, in March 1952 in a game against Manchester City, he earned the notoriety of being the first Claret and Blue to get his marching orders for nearly 20 years. His offence? Not a studs-up, two-footed challenge, not a professional foul or even two cautions: Elliott was sent off for giving his opponent a dirty look – or, as the ref wrote in his book, a 'look of intent'.

DRUNK IN CHARGE

Erratic decisions, a failure to keep up with play and a belligerent attitude – we've all seen refs like that at our local grounds, but those attending Tynec nad Labem's 2011 local derby against Jestrabi Lhota in the Czech Republic had good reason to doubt the whistle-carrier – he was wasted, wellied, wrecked …

Locals suspected Tomas Fidra's performance might not be tip-top when he climbed out of a taxi on arrival at the ground. 'His breath smelt like a brewery and he didn't hide the fact that he had been celebrating his birthday,' Karel Dusek, a Jestrabi official, told the *Lidove Noviny* newspaper. An accompanying photo showed the rat-arsed referee streaked with mud and pitch-marking white paint stains, the result of multiple stumbles and falls.

Fidra sent off three Jestrabi players during the match for no apparent reason, unless you count not agreeing to be his best friend, but the team played on. 'There's no rule which bans a drunk referee from taking charge of a match,' explained Dusek. 'If we had refused to continue to play, we could have been sanctioned.' Sportingly, the opposition agreed not to attack and the two sides amicably played out a 1-1 draw.

When the cops arrived, Fidra was found to have a 0.194 per cent blood alcohol level – about the highest a breathalyser can read. The game was later declared void and the ref left facing a suspension that would last until after his next birthday ...

MEMORIAL TO A DISMISSAL

German referee Rudolf Kreitlein refereed the 1966 European Cup final between Real Madrid and Partizan Belgrade, but remains most proud of his contribution to the Rattin controversy of that year (see pages 77–9) in the England versus Argentina World Cup quarter-final. A wall of Kreitlein's house was decorated with photos of the incident and, in 2006, still having never seen the match on TV, he contacted the FA to request a DVD.

Kreitlin takes his ball home after not being allowed to take a penalty at Wembley.

▦ HE JUST HAD TO GO

November 2007. A crunch Peterborough Sunday League Two clash sees Peterborough North End up against Royal Mail. The referee, 39-year-old Andy Wain, has a firm grip on the tightly fought match – right up until a 63rd-minute goal puts the Royal Mail side 2-1 ahead.

North End keeper Richard McGaffin is doing his nut, claiming a defender has been fouled. How will Andy react? Ignore him? Administer a quick ticking off? Give him a yellow card for dissent? Nope. Hearing the keeper moan, 'It's always the bloody same with you ref – we never get anything,' Andy hurls down his whistle, untucks his shirt and squares up to the player.

This is probably not a totally unheard-of occurrence in the hung-over, hurly-burly world of Sunday football, but what was about to happen certainly was. Suddenly coming to his senses, the referee stepped back and raised the red card. Those assuming he had dismissed the keeper were even more amazed when Andy himself began to leave the field with his head bowed.

'I squared up to the goalkeeper and it was totally unprofessional. If a player did that I would send him off, so I had to go,' explained the ref. He immediately apologised to the player and the teams – but still got a lifetime ban from his county FA.

▦ SCHARNER BEGS FOR RED

It's not often a player begs for a red card, but Wolves-baiting Baggie Paul Scharner went cap in hand to referee Mike Dean *after* being sent off in a Euro 2012 qualifying 4-4 draw between Austria and Belgium.

A body check against Paul Vertonghen had seen Scharner receive his marching orders, but the midfielder bore the referee no malice. 'It wasn't Mike Dean who decided to send me off, it was Mark Clattenburg the fourth official,' he told the *Daily Mirror*.

So when Dean subsequently turned up to officiate in a Black Country derby, the cheeky player asked him for a signed card – a memento of his first ever straight red. Dean was happy to oblige, even adding that rare sentiment from a whistle-blower, 'Sorry for the red card.'

▦ SEEING RED – AND SEEING STARS …

What do we think of diving? Awful isn't it, trying to get fellow professionals booked and sent off? It's underhand – unlike a good old shirt pull, an elbow to the face or a healthy honest studs-up challenge. In March 2012, a ref in a match in the Belgium lower league showed just how officials should deal with such nonsense.

The game in question was Templeuve versus Quévy. The home team's midfielder Julien Lecomte was already on a yellow when, as a corner came over, he collapsed on the ground, clutching his face as if he'd received the full force of a forward's elbow. The ref clearly wasn't taken in, but was forced to deal with the dramatic performance because the player just wouldn't get up.

Oh yes, he's good this one. Right down to being put on the stretcher – but the whistle-man had seen it all before. As they put the sheet over him – just like the DOAs at Holby City – the ref delivered the second yellow and then the dreaded red. Except, Templeuve was none the wiser. He really was out cold and, if replays confirming he had indeed been caught by an elbow weren't convincing enough, there were the hospital X-rays showing his three displaced vertebrae. Still he'll know next time, only go down if you're really hurt …

▦ TAKING THE MICK

In nearly 10 years of refereeing at the top of the English game, Gordon Hill never sent a player off in the Football League, FA Cup or League Cup. Famous for his amiable manner and for joining in with the on-field swearing, Hill did dismiss one player, the Lazio goalkeeper, during the second leg of Wolves' Anglo-Italian Cup tie in the Eternal City. In his autobiography, *Give A Little Whistle*, Hill describes how, after a tour of Rome's antiquities, he still had the greats of Renaissance art on the brain as he reffed the game. When cautioning the keeper, Hill asked his name and received the reply 'Michaelangelo!' Thinking the player was taking the mick, he sent him quickly on his way to the dressing room, only later learning he had actually given Michael Angelo Sulfaro his marching orders.

▥ THE RED CARDS THAT NEVER WERE

The 2006 South Western League match between Liskeard Athletic and Millbrook was getting pretty tasty. Millbrook defenders Andy Harris and Chris Graddon had both conceded penalties with professional fouls and Liskeard's Jimmy Alexander had gone in high and hard. All clear red card offences, they were all relieved to be given a stern warning from referee Paul Corcoran.

It wasn't until long after the game that the truth emerged: Corcoran confessed that he had left his yellow and red cards at home.

▥ THE JOKE'S ON YOU

Nowadays, we all know that Terry 'El Tel' Venables likes a laugh. After all, he invented the hilarious 'Thingummywig' (a hat with an attached wig that allowed women to leave the house wearing their curlers), does a mean Frank Sinatra impression and famously swapped jokes until the early hours with the likes of Dennis Wise and Gazza down at his club, Scribes West, in Kensington.

But, back in 1967, Venables was a 24-year-old in his second season at Spurs and his terrific sense of humour wasn't so renowned. As Tottenham enjoyed a 4-2 win over Fulham in February, Terry and Fulham's Fred Callaghan decided to have a joke at the expense of an over-officious referee, Mr H. New. As the two old pals staged a fake fight, the referee failed to see the funny side. Ignoring pleas from both players and their teammates, Mr New sent them both packing.

It's hard to see why Venables' sense of humour was not appreciated during his time at Spurs.

▦ THE THREE-CARD TRICK

Australia v. Croatia

World Cup, Group Match, Stuttgart, June 2006

'I will never forget the name of Josip Simunic for as long as I live. I'll probably be having nightmares about him forever more.' The man whose very name torments former referee Graham Poll was Croatia's talented but hard defender. His crime? To allow himself to be booked THREE times by the man rated England's finest referee.

It was always going to be a tense match, with Australia needing just a draw and Croatia needing a victory to progress to the next stage of the competition, and if added spice were needed there was a clash of loyalties with seven players of Croatian descent playing for Australia and three of the Croatian team who had spent their formative years in Australia, including Simunic.

By half-time Aussie Craig Moore's penalty had cancelled out Darijo Srna's superb free-kick opener for Croatia and the game had already been littered with meaty challenges from both sides. But the second half would see the heat turned up even further as Croatia regained the lead. In the 62nd minute, when Simunic bundled over Harry Kewell on the edge of the box, he became the third Croatian in Poll's book.

After Australia's equaliser – a Harry Kewell volley – in the 79th minute, the tension dial was racked up to 11. With five minutes left Simic and Emerton were dismissed for second yellow cards as Mr Poll showed great mathematical prowess. Then, with one minute left, Poll called Simunic over after a foul in the centre circle. As the crowd waited for the defender to start walking, the referee produced ... another yellow card. Poll admitted later that, confused by the Croatian's Aussie accent, he marked him down as Craig Moore, the Australian No. 3.

When the final whistle blew, the story reached its bizarre conclusion. Simunic approached Poll and, after a few words, received his third yellow and, at last, a red card.

For Poll, tipped to officiate in the final, the World Cup was over. Just a few days later he was sent home. The 43-year-old soon announced his retirement from international tournaments, but vowed to continue serving the Premier League. A year later, having endured a season of 'The World Cup and you f****ed it up' chants from crowds up and down the country, he packed his whistle away in its little box forever.

THE BATTLE OF ...

There should be a special collective noun for more than one red card. Perhaps a *Warnock* of Reds, an *Elleray* of expulsions or a *Rooney* of sendings off. But there isn't – so we'll have to settle for a 'disgrace of dismissals' in a collection of some of the best matches of mass red card action ...

▦ THE BATTLE OF BRAMALL LANE

Sheffield United v. West Bromwich Albion
March 2002

'There were 11 on the field and Warnock squealed, "fall over, fall over". So they all fell over and one was sent off ...' There aren't too many matches that get a 'terrace chant' written in tribute, but such was the farcical nature of West Brom's First Division tie with Sheffield United in 2002, it merited some kind of memorial.

Of course, with hindsight you might have seen something of a storm brewing. Albion's manager Gary Megson was a Sheffield Wednesday hero; Neil Warnock was, well, Neil Warnock, and both sides played a style of football that meant they were unlikely to top the fair play league. Add in some drama after United's George Santos had only recently recovered from a damaged eye-socket, an injury received however accidentally at the elbow of West Brom's Andy Johnson.

The referee always had things under control.

Still, we're all grown-ups and, besides, Santos was out of harm's way on the subs' bench. It took only nine minutes for United's goalie, Simon Tracy, to get dismissed, but no cause for alarm, it was just a technical offence for handling outside the penalty area. By the hour-mark the 10-man Blades were two behind and drifting towards an inevitable defeat. There didn't seem much for the Bramall Lane faithful to hang around for, but wait up – Santos is warming up ...

The Frenchman was on the pitch for 20 seconds. As Johnson picked up a pass in the middle of the field, Santos launched himself straight into the striker's ankles. Referee Eddie Wolstenholme's hand flew to his pocket just as quickly, but that wasn't enough to placate an angry group of players.

Sheffield's last sub Patrick Suffo had entered the action alongside Santos and managed to last an extra melee-filled 15 seconds before aiming an economic but devastating headbutt at Baggies defender Darren Moore. Now he was walking too. Down to eight men and with no subs left, the Blades had another half hour to play out.

Just after Albion notched their third on 77 minutes, United's Michael Brown hobbled off and a few minutes later his teammate Robert Ullathorne limped to the sidelines. Six-man Sheffield had reached the magic FIFA number and the match had to be abandoned.

'If we are called back to Sheffield, we will kick off, then walk off the pitch,' WBA boss Megson said after the game. Warnock later went for a more personal angle, saying of his fellow manager, 'I wouldn't piss on him if he was on fire.' The league ruled that the 3-0 result would stand and fined United. Neither Santos nor Suffo would ever appear in the famous red and white stripes again.

THE BATTLE OF SALTERGATE

Chesterfield v. Plymouth Argyle

February 1997

'It's the first time in my career I've had to deal with anything like that, and it was quite frightening,' referee Richard Poulain told the BBC. 'The two No. 6s were having a boxing match in the net and the two

No. 8s were exchanging blows outside the area.' Poulain was explaining just how he became the first Football League referee to send off five players in one match.

The 1997 Chesterfield and Plymouth encounter had been a pretty mundane affair. Argyle had Ronnie Mauge dismissed in the 36th minute for a high two-footed tackle but tempers did not seem over-frayed. Then with just two minutes left, the whole thing exploded. The touch paper was the errant elbow of Chesterfield's Darren Carr, which caught legendary keeper Bruce Grobbelaar (in the midst of his match-fixing trial at the time).

'It was an incredible scene,' related Poulain. 'A mass brawl began, with players connecting with each other, just before the end of the match. It was going crazy.' It didn't help that 20 or so fans joined in, followed by a handful of well-meaning stewards. By the time the dust had settled, Poulain had sent off the obvious offenders – two from each team – and so entered the history books.

Plymouth, who were leading the game 2-1, played out the closing minutes with a reported 3-3-1 formation and a goalkeeper still seeing stars. And, for once, both managers seem to take the ref's side, agreeing that Poulain had really had no option.

▦ THE BATTLE OF THE BOMBONERA

Boca Juniors v. Sporting Cristal

March 1971

Heaven knows how high a horse today's TV and radio experts would have climbed on to if they'd have witnessed Boca Juniors versus Sporting Cristal of Peru in their Copa Libertadores tie of 1971.

Boca, who needed to win to progress in the tournament, had taken a 2-0 lead, but by the 70th minute had been pegged back to 2-2. But that really isn't important. With four minutes left, Boca midfielder Roberto Rogel took a tumble in the Cristal area as Fernando Mellán attempted to clear the ball. The Boca players yelled for a spot kick while the Peruvians took exception to the perceived dive. Then it all kicked off.

Boca's Rubén Suñé threw the first punch at Alberto Gallardo, who responded with a flying kick to the face. Suddenly virtually every player on the field wanted some – one player was chasing another with a corner flag, while Mellán received the full force of a boot in the face as he lay on the floor. As spectators and riot police joined the fray, officials abandoned the match.

Later, when referee Alejandro Otero consulted his notebook, it transpired that 19 players had been sent off – every outfield man with the exception of Boca defender Julio Meléndez, who happened to be Peruvian himself. Campos, with a broken nose, and Mellán, whose skull was fractured in the battering, were taken to one hospital, while Suñé was driven to another for seven facial stitches courtesy of Gallardo's size 11. The rest of the players spent the night at the local prison where they reportedly kissed and made up and had a rare ol' time, but were released in the morning to face some hefty bans. And if that wasn't enough, the mother of Cristal defender Orlando de la Torre died of a heart attack while watching the melee on TV.

▦ IT'S ALL JUST HANDBAGS!

Red cards are rare in women's football: mistimed tackles are not so brutal, there are fewer histrionics and the game in general is played in a more sporting atmosphere. But there are exceptions ...

Blackburn Rovers Ladies had a pretty impeccable sporting reputation. That is until January 2007, when a tense cup-tie with Chelsea saw two Blackburn players sent off and the police called to protect the ref from a baying 200-strong crowd.

Then, in October 2008, another tense match, this time in the Premier League Cup against Portsmouth, saw them reduced to seven players. Referee Lee Taylor dished out four reds: Natalie Brewer and Natalie Preston both got the double yellow, Jenna Carroll saw red for retaliation and hat-trick hero Katie Anderton walked after some 'unladylike' words to the match official.

Just when the men's side had finally managed to escape the 'Blackeye Rovers' tag ...

▦ THE BATTLE OF BERNE

Hungary v. Brazil

June 1954

'I thought it was going to be the greatest game I'd ever see,' Arthur Ellis told the *Independent*. 'Whether politics and religion had something to do with it I don't know, but they behaved like animals. It was a disgrace.'

Some might remember Arthur Ellis as the avuncular, elderly officiator of BBC's *It's a Knockout*, but before that – in the post-war period – he was recognised as one of the best referees in the world. As such, he was selected to run the rule over the most eagerly awaited international ever.

The quarter-finals of the 1954 World Cup had pitched together not only the tournament's two highest scorers, but the great entertainers of the time: Hungary, whose free-flowing football was revolutionising the game, and Brazil, a team of audaciously skilful individuals.

It didn't turn out exactly like that. After the Hungarians had taken a 3-1 lead early in the second half, the Brazilians seemed to decide the game was up. From now on it was to be a physical battle, one the East Europeans were only too happy to join. While every tackle seemed to go over the top, elsewhere on the pitch personal feuds were being played out. *The Times* would report, 'Never in my life have I seen such cruel tackling, the cutting down of opponents as if with a scythe, followed by threatening attitudes and sly jabs when officialdom was engaged elsewhere.'

Ellis was to award 43 free kicks in all, but managed to keep all the players on the field until Nilton Santos and Josef Bozsik, a member of Hungary's parliament, swapped punches and he had no options left. Both teams had completely lost it. Humberto went for Koscis and was left begging to be allowed to partake in the last four minutes of the free-for-all. When he eventually walked, Koscis got up to make it 4-2 to Hungary and the result was sealed.

For Ellis it was finally over, but not for the teams. The players clashed in the tunnel, with fans, press and officials all joining in. Hungary's coach Gustav Sebes got hit by a bottle and the great Puskas, who had sat in the stand all match nursing an injury, was rumoured to have wielded a broken bottle as the fight spilled into the dressing rooms.

Puskas's autobiography added little: 'Who had come best out of the extra time in the dressing room it was impossible to decide,' he wrote. 'There had been no referee.' Ellis, his job done, had long since locked himself away.

THE BATTLE OF MONTEVIDEO

Racing Club v. Celtic
November 1967

If the film censors rated football matches this one would be down as an 18 and no mistake. Celtic, as European Champions, had beaten Argentina's Racing Club 1-0 at Hampden in the first leg of the 1967 World Club Championship. The second leg in Buenos Aires had taken things a step further as Celtic keeper Ronnie Simpson suffered a head wound from a missile and winger Jimmy Johnstone was kicked more times than the ball. Worse still, a 2-1 victory for the South Americans meant a third match was needed to separate the teams. The Celtic players and board might have been happy to call it a day, but Jock Stein was desperate for his team to be proclaimed the best club in the world.

The third tie was played in Montevideo, Uruguay, three days later – and this time, the Glaswegians weren't prepared to turn the other cheek. Early in the game, as Johnstone was again scythed down, a melee ensued resulting in Alfio Basile and Bobby Lennox being sent off. Jock Stein ordered his skipper back on the pitch, but when riot police with swords approached him, Lennox decided to disobey his boss for once.

Heaven knows how the first half passed without any more early baths, but the second period descended into pure violence. When the umpteenth foul on Johnstone produced a flying elbow in retaliation, Jinky found himself dismissed – no doubt half relieved to be out of the firing line.

Striker John Hughes was next to follow the ref's pointing finger. Hyped up from start, Hughes had closed down the Racing keeper and, in plain view, threw a jab at his stomach. The goalie went down as if he'd got a belter from Sonny Liston so, for good measure, Hughes followed it up with a kick to the groin.

Bertie Auld, the hard-as-nails guy in this team of hardmen, didn't want to be left out, running a full 15 yards to nail an opponent. He should have been Celtic's fourth man off, but Auld stood his ground. Even the riot police couldn't shift him, so he stayed. While all hell broke loose around Auld, Tommy Gemmell took the opportunity to unleash a kick that almost sent Ayala's crown jewels right up to his throat. Ironically, Racing's Ruilli was then sent off for what was one of the softest fouls of the match.

Somewhere amid the scrapping, Racing's Cárdenas scored a humdinger 30-yard strike to win. Celtic had lost the match and the moral high ground. The Racing players were each given a new car, while the Celtic board fined their team eight weeks wages each and scratched Jock Stein's name off the New Year's Honours list.

Racing goalscorer Cárdenas' cries of 'I haven't even got cramp' went unheard.

THE BATTLE OF SANTIAGO

Chile v. Italy
June 1962

David Coleman's introduction still whets the appetite: 'The game you're about to see is the most stupid, appalling, disgusting and disgraceful exhibition of football possibly in the history of the game.'

British referee Ken Aston (see page 10) took charge, or to be more accurate, dressed in black and ran around with a whistle – but he wasn't solely at fault. You could equally blame the two Italian journalists whose articles on Santiago and the low morals of its women provoked incandescent ire in the host nation, or both teams' willingness to resort to violence at the slightest provocation. Aston later wrote, 'I wasn't reffing a football match. I was acting as an umpire in military manoeuvres.'

It took 30 seconds for Aston to award the first free kick, eight minutes for Italy's Giorgio Ferrini to be dismissed and another eight for local police to drag him off the pitch. Then things got out of hand: Chilean Leonel Sanchez, the son of a professional boxer, got bored of Mario David's incessant fouls and laid him out. Aston, seemingly unwilling to punish the Chileans in their capital city, let events take their course. So, minutes later, in retaliation, David took off with a flying kung-fu style kick at Sanchez's neck, at which point Aston did act – sending David to join his teammate in the bath.

Scuffles and spitting bouts interrupted the game, the police came on the pitch three times, and then Sanchez broke Humberto Maschio's nose with a left hook ('I say, that was one of the neatest left hooks I've ever seen!' – Coleman again!), but Aston had gone back into his shell. When the final whistle went he turned tail and headed for the dressing room – leaving the players still scrapping it out on the pitch. Oh – and Chile won 2-0.

EVEN THE BEST

→ • • • • • • • • • • • • • • •

Having more skill in your little toe than the rest of your team put together does not exempt you from the ref's scrutiny. In fact, being one of the best in the world probably vastly increases the likelihood of seeing red. These are the players it's worth winding up, the ones who are getting niggled, pulled and clattered throughout the game and whose scalp the man with the cards may regard as a feather in his cap.

▦ BOBBY MOORE

The England captain, gentleman and, if you listen to West Ham fans, latter-day saint, was renowned for his perfectly timed tackles, calm temperament and self-discipline – even remembering to wipe his sweaty hands on his shirt before receiving the World Cup from the Queen. A good bet for an unblemished career à la Gary Lineker you might think, but investigation reveals that even St Robert had to peer down the ref's armpit on two occasions.

His first was in a league match at Maine Road in 1962 with literally the last kick of the game. Moore, who had made his England debut earlier that season, had had his hackles raised by young Manchester City winger David Wagstaffe. Having received no protection from the ref, Moore, ever the pro, waited until the players trooped off at full time to exact his own retribution. Unfortunately, the incident was spotted by the officials and Moore was dismissed for the first time in his career.

Then, in October 1976, just after Wagstaffe had made his own bid for red card record-breaking fame (see page 72), Moore was to see one of the shiny new red cards in person. By then he was at Fulham, who had a feisty encounter with Bolton in the League Cup. After the ref had added six minutes injury time for time wasting, Bolton only went and equalised.

The Fulham players went ballistic, chief among them, the former England captain to whom ref McNally chose to show one of his freshly made cards. To prevent events descending into anarchy, Fulham manager Alec Stock withdrew his team from the pitch. McNally followed him, along with two policemen, threatening to award the tie to Bolton if they weren't ready to start in two minutes time. Sure enough, back they trotted without Sir Bobby and played out the draw.

▦ JOHANN CRUYFF

Acknowledged as the best player in the world once Pelé had gone west (to New York Cosmos), Johann Cruyff would come to epitomise everything that was great about the 'Total Football'-playing Holland team of the 1970s. His early international days, however, were mired in the kind of controversy at which the Dutch seem to excel.

Before he'd even made his international debut, Cruyff was already feted as the saviour of Dutch football. His team, Ajax, had been particularly protective of the skinny young thing, but in September 1966 they finally relented and allowed their teenage prodigy to be selected by the national side for a Euro 68 qualifier against Hungary.

Unsurprisingly Cruyff impressed everyone, scoring once in a 2-2 draw and, much to the Dutch FA's chagrin, Ajax would not let him play again for a couple of months, and he did not start again until the friendly against Czechoslovakia in November. This time the future Dutch Master lost it completely with East German referee Rudolph Glockner who claimed – although Cruyff still denies it – that the Dutchman actually hit him. Glockner dismissed the 19-year-old star, who became the first ever Dutch player to be sent off in 61 years of international football. He was banned for a year by the Dutch FA – a decision that set Cruyff against his national team and ultimately prevented the blossoming Holland team from qualifying for the 1970 World Cup finals.

▦ GEORGE BEST

One of the greatest players in the world if you listen to old geezers and watch the five minutes of dribbling that the BBC always put out – what would you reckon on Bestie ever getting the big red one? (If you've read page 72 you're not allowed to answer.)

Let's see: hot-headed – check; persistently kicked and buffered on and off the ball – check; a creative genius – check; red-haired – er, well no, but three out of four ain't bad. Of course he did ...

1968: In the first leg of the World Club Championship against Estudiantes in Buenos Aires, Manchester United, winners of that year's European Cup, had been kicked to bits and had Nobby Stiles sent off for retaliation. Back at Old Trafford, Best got sick of the treatment by his marker Medina. He recalled in his autobiography, *Blessed*, 'Finally, near the end [the referee] decided to book him, but

I thought he had waited far too long. I chinned the guy as he was being booked … It was the most satisfying red card I've ever had.' For good measure George gobbed at him on the way off and both players had to be escorted to the dressing rooms.

1969: Already booked by future World Cup final referee Jack Taylor in the League Cup semi-final against Manchester City, George approaches the ref at the end of the match and flips the ball from his hands. Caught on TV, he receives a £100 fine and is suspended for four weeks. In his first game back he scores six in United's 8-2 FA Cup defeat of Northampton Town.

The lonely walk to the dressing room – with only a magnum of bubby and a partially naked Miss World to look forward to…

1970: George gives it the 'Turf and Surf' in a match against Scotland. A bravura hissy fit saw the Belfast Boy, in the green of Northern Ireland, getting his marching orders for flinging mud and spitting at the ref. Martin O'Neill, who was at the match as a boy, later told the *Daily Mail*, 'I never saw a player want to get sent off as much.' Best was fined £250 and suspended for six weeks.

1972: In the great 1971-72 clampdown, George is sent for an early one in a match against Chelsea for calling top referee Norman Burtenshaw 'a ****ing disgrace'. Supposedly the ref asked his name and getting the answer 'Best' replied 'Initial?' George would escape a lengthy ban when he convinced the FA disciplinary authorities that he hadn't been swearing at the ref, but at his teammate Willie Morgan!

Bestie wasn't quite finished there. He'd see red again for Northern Ireland in Sofia in 1973 when he lashed out in retaliation at a defender and when he almost became a record-breaker with Fulham at the Dell (see page 72).

▦ JIMMY GREAVES

Greavsie first got his marching orders in Spurs' pioneering European days. In 1963, on the way to becoming the first English club to win a European title, Tottenham journeyed to Yugoslavia for the first leg of the Cup-Winners' Cup semi-final against OFK Belgrade.

Those 1960s away ties were brutal affairs and this was a peach because Spurs, with the likes of the bruising Bobby Smith and ironman Dave Mackay, were ready to give as good as they got. Greaves, of course, was cut from a different cloth. In the second half of the match, the Belgrade defender Krivokuca was winded by a flailing Bobby Smith elbow. Raising his bulk from the ground he went for the first Spurs player he could see – Greavsie. Well, as the man says, it's a funny old game.

Krivokuca swung a punch but the England striker ducked like a flyweight, bobbing up to deliver his own haymaker – into the

Belgrade air. As the players were pulled apart, it became apparent that the ref had noticed Greaves' effort but failed to spot his sparring partner's flying fist. Jimmy walked alone.

Tottenham went on to record a famous 2-1 victory, but Greaves would miss the next leg and was suitably miffed. In his autobiography *Greavsie*, he tells how Spurs trainer Cecil Poynton provided a great postscript. 'It's ya own fault,' he recalls Poynton saying. 'Ya shuddana reacted like that. Ya the first Spurs player to be sent off in a game since 1928. You've blemished the record of this fine club.' Thus chastised, Greaves could only ask who the player who shared his disgrace was. 'Me!' replied the trainer.

▦ DIEGO MARADONA

World Cups would make Diego Maradona both hero and villain. The teenage prodigy would miss the glorious home victory in 1978, but future tournaments would see him emerge as one of the world's best players, perform one of the most notorious acts of cheating ever, score one of the tournament's best ever goals, single-handedly drag his team to the final, get sent home in disgrace after failing a drugs test – and execute one of the funniest red card offences in World Cup history.

Having been the subject of a world-record signing from Boca Juniors to Barcelona, millions awaited Argentina's new star, 21-year-old Diego Maradona's appearance in the 1982 World Cup in Spain. He stuttered in their opening game, but they weren't disappointed for long. The next game, against Hungary, saw him not only claim two goals in Argentina's 4-0 victory with a diving header and a fierce drive, but run the match.

In the first match of their second round group, Italy's Gentile showed just how to shackle Maradona, employing a combination of superb man-marking and devious off-the-ball tugging and pulling. As Argentina went down 2-1 to the eventual champions, El Diego was left frustrated. His temper hadn't boiled over yet, but there was still a match to go …

In Barcelona, Argentina needed to beat a Brazil team inspired by Falcao, Socrates and Zico to keep their hopes alive. But where Italy shackled them with negativity, Brazil stunned them with brilliance – three superb goals left their rivals open-mouthed and Maradona's World Cup in its death throes.

Time was ticking away. How could he leave his mark on these finals? Brazilian substitute João Batista had been on the pitch for only two minutes, but having won the ball with a nasty challenge, he came face to face with 10 stone of fuming muscle. With a kick to Batista's crown jewels as elegant as anything Maradona had shown so far, he exited the tournament three minutes before the rest of his teammates.

Later Maradona excused his attack, claiming he'd got the wrong guy, 'I lashed out, kicking Batista in the balls. But it was meant for Falcao ...' At least he never stooped to call it 'the groin-kick of God.'

▒ PELÉ

Named the greatest ever footballer by everyone from FIFA to the Women's Institute (with the notable exception of one Diego Armando Maradona who seemed to think the accolade should go to someone else), the Black Pearl is the nearest thing the world game has to a saint. And yet, for all his goalscoring, World Cup-winning, own-half shooting, children's-charity raising, erectile-dysfunction fighting heroics, he too got to see the raised arm of the man in black.

Pelé was dismissed on a few occasions for his Brazilian club side, Santos. One notable occasion came in May 1959 in a match against São Paulo rivals Juventus. Although only 19, Pelé was already a star and a few days after the game he was invited to referee a game between Santos and São Paulo officials – including the weekend's offending referee, Olten Ayres de Abreu. Needless to say, sweet revenge was enacted as a whistle-touting Pelé made sure Olten was sent packing.

It takes a brave referee to send the most popular player on the planet to the dressing room, so step forward one Guillermo 'Chato' Velazquez. In 1969, Santos were in Bogotá, Colombia for a 'friendly' against the Colombian Olympic team. The Colombians had been kicking and insulting Pelé and his black teammates Edu and Lima all game long with no protection from the belligerent Chato. As a frustrated Lima complained once too often, Chato went ballistic and sent him off for dissent. Pelé took up where his teammate had finished and was soon ordered to follow him.

End of story? Not quite ... the 'home' crowd had come to see the world's greatest footballer, not some haughty official, and they threw cushions and anything else they could get their hands on down on to the pitch. Baton-wielding police surrounded Chato to protect him and calm matters down, but the crowd's chants just got louder.

Fearing a full-scale riot, the police sent an official to the dressing room to ask Pelé to return to the pitch immediately. He emerged from the tunnel to find the game suspended, the touchline lined with armed police and a seething Chato being escorted out of the stadium.

Funny how Dennis Wise was sent off 13 times, but the same thing never happened to him ...

▦ LIONEL MESSI

Argentina had spent nigh on 20 years looking for the new Maradona: Ortega, Riquelme, Aimar had all been touted, but ultimately disappointed. Lionel Messi was next on the conveyor belt. In June 2005 he had almost single-handedly won his country the Under-20 World Cup and was ready to step up to the senior team.

But Argentina were nervous. Although never expressing any doubts about his intentions to play for the country of his birth, Messi had moved to Spain at the age of 13 and was still eligible to play for their national side. For Argentina, a friendly against Hungary in August 2005, provided the perfect opportunity to blood the 18-year-old and make him an Albiceleste forever.

After 63 minutes of the match, with Argentina leading 2-1, coach José Pekerman withdrew Maxi Lopez and gave the most exciting talent of his generation his international debut. Immediately, Messi was assured and comfortable on the ball. With his second touch, he ghosted past Hungarian Vilmos Vanczák, who grabbed him by his pristine No. 18 shirt. As Messi pushed back to wriggle free, the defender went to ground clutching his face. Referee Markus Merk was right on hand to deliver the red card. Messi had been on the pitch for 40 seconds!

GIANFRANCO ZOLA

It was the present that the great Gianfranco Zola must have wanted for his 28th birthday. With 65 minutes gone and Italy trailing 1-0 to Nigeria, who were the surprise package of the 1994 World Cup, coach Arrigo Sacchi gave the popular Sardinian his World Cup debut and the chance to turn his nation's fortunes around.

However, referee Brizio Carter (see page 122–3) had a little present of his own tucked away and, like an excited child, just couldn't wait to deliver it. Only 10 minutes had elapsed when a burst of pace took the player they call the 'Magic Box' into the area. As he toppled in a challenge with Augustine Eguavoen, the Italian was maybe a little over optimistic in claiming a penalty, but, getting back to his feet, he was ready to pursue the defender to the touchline to exact some kind of revenge. Zola's half-stamp, half-tackle missed the Nigerian, but didn't stop him collapsing in agony. Brizio Carter didn't need another chance. Out came his present – in red.

Zola crumpled to the ground repeating 'No, no, no' in a mantra of anger, shame and sheer disbelief. He made it a yard off the field, but couldn't go any further. It was the most pitiful after-card performance you'll ever see: Nigerian players, pitchside photographers, peanut sellers all taking their opportunity to console him. But that was it – and Zola would never again appear in a World Cup finals fixture.

As for Italy – their fortunes were turned round by someone else. Roberto Baggio's goals (one with two minutes left and another in extra-time) ensured a famous victory and the Divine Ponytail would inspire them all the way to the final.

10 minutes! At least Gianfranco's pristine kit wouldn't need washing.

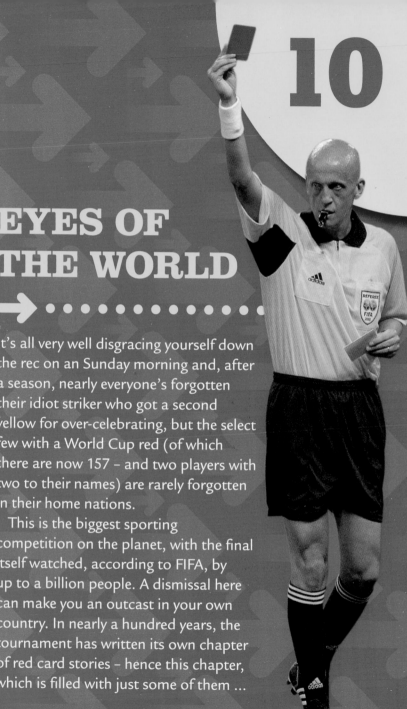

EYES OF
THE WORLD

→ • • • • • • • • • • •

It's all very well disgracing yourself down the rec on an Sunday morning and, after a season, nearly everyone's forgotten their idiot striker who got a second yellow for over-celebrating, but the select few with a World Cup red (of which there are now 157 – and two players with two to their names) are rarely forgotten in their home nations.

This is the biggest sporting competition on the planet, with the final itself watched, according to FIFA, by up to a billion people. A dismissal here can make you an outcast in your own country. In nearly a hundred years, the tournament has written its own chapter of red card stories – hence this chapter, which is filled with just some of them …

▦ A FIRST IN THE FINALS

Romania v. Peru
World Cup, Pool 3, Montevideo, Uruguay, 1930
On the second ever day of the inaugural World Cup, in front of what remains a record for the smallest ever finals crowd (estimated at around 300), Chilean referee Alberto Warken ordered the first ever dismissal of the competition.

After Desu had put the Europeans ahead in the first minute, the game had disintegrated into a series of brawls and feuds. Tempers were further fuelled when, on 38 minutes, Romanian right back Steiner had his leg broken in a collision with Peruvian De Las Casas. It was said to be an accident but the Romanians – with no substitutions then available – set out to equal the numbers by crocking an opponent or provoking a Peruvian into getting sent off.

Half-time did little to calm the teams down, and in the 56th minute, in an attempt to regain some control, the referee dismissed Peru's skipper and centre-half Plácido Galindo. Even then he needed the help of the Uruguayan police to get him off the pitch. A couple of minutes later Peru equalised, but their 10 men failed to hold out and conceded another two. However, it was Galindo who had made the real history that day.

▦ A FINNEY THING HAPPENED ON THE WAY TO THE SEMIS

West Germany v. Uruguay
World Cup, quarter-final, Hillsborough, 1966
It seems hard to comprehend, but after England's historic World Cup victory in 1966 there were some people who weren't singing the praises of Geoff Hurst, Bobby Moore or Sir Alf's Wingless Wonders. In particular, the South Americans were nursing grievances, imagined and real …

On the same day that England were taking on 'animals' Argentina (see pages 77–9), a couple of hundred miles up north another feisty Europe versus South America battle was underway. West Germany, so far looking the best team in the tournament, were taking on an as yet unbeaten Uruguayan XI. The two sides, both having already shown their mastery of football's dark arts, were playing for a place in the semi-final under the gaze of English referee, Jim Finney.

In the early minutes, Finney got on the wrong side of the South Americans when he ignored a blatant handball by German defender Schnellinger under the German crossbar. Seemingly unconcerned as the Germans dished out the rough stuff, then writhed and rolled under every Uruguayan challenge (nothing ever changes!), Finney really began to get their goat.

Still, the game was tight, Haller's 11th-minute deflection having given the Germans the lead, until the 50th minute when Uruguay captain Horacio Troche dealt out some justice of his own, kicking Emmerich in the belly then, having received his marching orders, slapping Uwe Seeler for laughing. Obviously unsure he'd leave the field, Finney personally escorted him to the touchline.

Five minutes later, forward Hector Silva, irritated by yet another dying fly impersonation from Haller, gave him something real to complain about by scraping his studs down the German's legs. This time Finney left it to a brace of British bobbies to make sure the Uruguay forward played no further part in the game. Uruguay's nine men were no match for such a strong West German side, who proceeded to knock another three past them and coast into the final at Wembley.

Over on the other side of the world, they were frothing ... West Germany through with an English ref, England through with a German ref – both against South American opposition? 'Conspiracy!' they cried and laid siege to the English ambassador's residence in Montevideo.

▦ COLD WAR COLLISION

Soviet Union v. West Germany
World Cup, semi-final, Goodison Park, 1966
For all the fuss and bother over the South Americans (see page 79), possibly the crucial dismissal of 1966 came in the semi-finals. The Soviet Union reached the last four with their reputation greatly

enhanced by winning every match. In Yashin, Shesternev, Voronin and Chislenko, they had players who could take them all the way to Wembley. Up against them were a skilful but – as they had shown in the quarter-final against Uruguay – very physical West German side.

The game was not pretty. One newspaper reported that the sides went at each other 'as if they were at war' and when Banichevski was taken out of the game with a crude foul there was a brief mass brawl. The Soviets' inside-right, Igor Chislenko, had already been on the end of some agricultural challenges from Schlesinger – and a tackle that left him limping led to Haller putting West Germany ahead a few minutes before half-time. A minute later, frustrated by yet another stiff challenge that appeared to leave marks on his knee, Igor snapped and kicked out at Held, who milked it like a Thomas Hardy dairymaid.

Even with Chislenko dispatched by excellently named referee Concetto Lo Bello, the 10-man Soviet team were well in the game until Franz Beckenbauer's beautiful 20-yard strike settled the affair. Is it possible a certain Russian linesman was watching, cursing the luck of the Germans and working out a way to get revenge?

▦ GONE IN 50 SECONDS

Uruguay v. Scotland
World Cup, Group E, Neza, Mexico, 1986
Like most of their trips to the World Cup finals, Scotland's 1986 adventure ended quickly, but on this occasion their qualification was not in vain. Scotland would gain a place in the record books thanks to Uruguay's Sergio Batista, who clattered into the back of Gordon Strachan just 56 seconds into their game and earned the fastest ever red card in the history of the finals.

By that point in the group stage, Scotland were just making up the numbers, while Uruguay needed a draw to progress. They'd got a good draw against West Germany in their opener, but once Miguel Bossio had been sent off after 19 minutes they'd capitulated to the Danes, losing 6-1 second time out. They didn't seem to have learned

The unacceptable face of football. Strachan sports the red mullet and takes the inevitable punishment.

much when Batista got his first-minute marching orders against Scotland, but through a physical and ultra-defensive approach they got their point.

Scotland's coach at the time was none other than a young Alex Ferguson. He was fuming – a sight we'd all come to get used to. After Uruguay coach Borras had claimed his team were victims of a refereeing conspiracy and even called ref Joel Quiniou 'a murderer', Fergie let rip on the Uruguay team, their tactics, their culture, the amount of vowels in their name and more. 'It's a shambles, a complete shambles,' he ranted. 'I mean, it's not just a part of football, it's the whole bloody attitude of the nation. You can see that attitude there. They have no respect for other people's dignity. It's a disgrace what they did. Their behaviour turns the game into a complete farce ... But there you are, we're out of the World Cup. I can't even say good luck to Uruguay because I don't think they deserve it.'

Well, they didn't get any either, going out 1-0 to Argentina in the next round; but at least they finished that match with 11 men.

▦ MASSING WASN'T MESSING

Cameroon v. Argentina
World Cup, Group B, Milan, 1990

Red card heroes are few and far between. You might love your thuggish defender who sees red for knocking your local rivals' star forward unconscious, or your defender who sacrifices himself with a last-ditch outside-the-area professional foul – but you know the rest of the world are tutting and looking heavenwards. Benjamin Massing, however, manages to sit in the top 20 for a brutal challenge that was cheered across the world – except in Argentina!

In the opening game of the 1990 World Cup finals in Milan, reigning World Cup holders Argentina faced a totally unfancied Cameroon team. Argentina were still inspired by Diego Maradona but much of the flair of the previous decade had been replaced with cynicism and defensive tactics. In contrast, the Cameroonians were mostly unknown and even included a 38-year old named Roger Milla on the subs' bench. Oh how we laughed at their 'naivety' and 'unsophisticated approach'!

On the hour there was still no score although Cameroon had kicked lumps out of an opposition more used to dishing it out than taking it. Then, as the lightning-paced Caniggia finally broke free of the Africans' defence, he was deliberately clipped by Kana-Biyik. The defender was ordered off and we waited for Argentina to make hay. Just five minutes later, the deadlock was broken, but amazingly by the 10 men – Argentina keeper Nero Pumpido making a right mess of Omam-Biyik's gentle header.

Cameroon continued to take no prisoners as they strove to hold onto their lead. With just two minutes to go, Caniggia again picked up the ball inside his own half. Setting off on a characteristic run, he skipped over a half-hearted tackle and crossed the halfway line in full flight. The next challenge – a dangerous lunge from the side – would have been enough to earn a booking. The ref played on though, as Caniggia somehow managed to ride it and, struggling to regain his balance, continued his run.

Benjamin Massing had watched and learned ... Caniggia had only just recovered his full stride when the defender repeated his teammate's assault, this time with double the force – enough to lose his own boot and leave the striker wondering where the juggernaut had come from. Massing left the field, walking round the pitch celebrating like a boxer after a knockout punch as his team saw out an historic victory.

Why do we love it? Argentina receiving a taste of their own medicine? The underdogs striking back? Or maybe it was just the kind of challenge that leaves you open-mouthed at the sheer gall of it – the tremendous physical force and a certain elegance that flouted every code of sportsmanship but somehow seemed so right?

A SPAT, A SPIT AND AN INTERNATIONAL INCIDENT

Netherlands v. West Germany
World Cup, Second Round, Milan, 1990

As international rivalries go, Netherlands v. Germany is up there among the fiercest – driven by proximity, some tasty previous matches and a certain world war. The iconic moment of their animosity came when Frank Rijkaard and Rudi Völler – both sporting hilarious perm and 'tache combos – confronted each other in a tense World Cup tie in 1990.

A reconciliation breakfast at Frank's. Rudi avoided asking just what was floating in the orange juice ...

Only 20 minutes had passed when Frank's late tackle impeded Völler's progress. Naturally the German made the most of it and Rijkaard was left looking at a yellow card that would mean missing the quarter-final. Miffed, the Dutchman retreated to his position, pausing only briefly to fly a ball of spittle past Völler's face.

As the two awaited the free-kick Frank repeated his trick, but this time the phlegm projectile hit the target ... Völler's reaction earning him a yellow. Moments later, as Völler only just pulled out of a lunging challenge on goalkeeper Hans van Breukelen, Rijkaard was first on the scene. Forced to sort out the ensuing melee, referee Juan Loustau lost patience with the squabblers and sent them both packing.

Frank, however, was hawking up one final flob and this one was the best. A direct hit, it hung glinting like a Christmas bauble on Rudi's tight curls as the striker decided to leg it for the showers and a double dose of Head & Shoulders.

Out on the Dutch-German border, the incident led to rioting raiding parties, while dark rumours spread of racist remarks sparking the incident. The irony was that Frank, who himself put paid to the rumours, and Rudi were friends and both were renowned as two of the nicest players around. As Ulrich Hesse-Lichtenburger relates in his fine book *Tor! A History of German Football*, 'Five months later, when Milan played Roma, Rijkaard apologised and said he'd lost his head, explaining he'd been under emotional pressure, having separated from his wife shortly before the World Cup.'

▦ A RED IN ROME

Argentina v. West Germany
World Cup final, Rome, 1990

After a tournament that had seen the emerging Cameroon, Gazza's England and Baggio's Italy, it was the final no one really wanted. Argentina, defensive and dirty and now missing four suspended players, would meet a West German team who had shown some flair, but mostly for throwing themselves in the air at every challenge. It was going to be dire ...

The two teams didn't disappoint in a match where nothing happened; the game was saved only by not only the first ever red card in a World Cup final but also the second. The first was stereotype-tastic. On 64 minutes, Jürgen Klinnsman broke down the right wing and, not yet at full speed, angled his run towards the penalty area. Argentine substitute Pedro Monzón, who had only come on at half-time, jumped in with a professional foul disguised as a clumsy challenge. But in the land of subterfuge, the flying German is king. Klinsmann took off Fosbury Flop style, landed, flipped like a beetle, rolled over three times and gripped his head. He hadn't even got through half his performance by the time referee Edgardo Codesal had waved his red card.

When Andreas Brehme's 84th-minute penalty appeared to have sealed the match, the Argentinians became slightly peeved. As Jürgen Köhler began to carry the ball from the touchline for a goal kick, forward Gustavo Dezotti approached him. Suddenly we were watching rugby. Kohler executed a neat sidestep to evade his opponent, but Dezotti grabbed him round the throat and pulled him down. High tackle? Codesal, though 40 yards away, thought so and flamboyantly flourished his red card. As Argentinians clattered into the referee from behind like a train crash – first Troglio, then Serrizuela and finally Maradona, they were lucky not to join him.

After 14 dismissal-free finals, the red cards, like the match itself, were a disappointment – low on controversy, brutality, farce and laughs. Still, it was a start ...

▦ KEV GETS IT WRONG

Brazil v. USA
World Cup, Round of 16, Stanford, 1994
Kevin Keegan: 'I didn't think he had done that much wrong. He was being held ... he was being fouled first. I mean it's ...'

Alan Parry: 'An elbow.'

Brazil's Leonardo wasn't, as they say, 'that kind of player'. But his assault on USA midfielder Tab Ramos earned him the second longest ban ever and left the American in hospital for the next three months.

Viewers in Britain were shocked at the force with which the Brazilian had swung his elbow into Tab's face, but were even more gob-smacked by Kev's inability to see the offence. As the world winced, slow-motion replays found Keegan agonisingly extricating himself from a losing argument.

What happened next? Leonardo got a four-match ban, Brazil went on to win the World Cup without him (but he still got a medal, having played in the first four games, well, three and a bit), and Keegan went on to embarrass himself further by saying there was 'no way' England could lose to Romania at France '98, predicting David Batty would score his penalty against Argentina and, of course, his 'love it' rant. Ironically, Leonardo would turn up as an expert himself on the BBC's 2006 World Cup panel.

NEED A RED? GET CARTER

Respected Mexican referee Arturo Brizio Carter made his World Cup debut with the 1994 opener between Germany and Bolivia in Chicago, sending off Bolivian substitute Marco Etcheverry for a kick on Lothar Matthäus (who could resist?) just four minutes after coming on. Days later, he upped the stakes by giving a red to Cameroon's Rigobert Song against Brazil in San Francisco, making the 17-year-old Song the youngest player to be sent off in the World Cup finals. He completed his USA '94 hat-trick by dismissing another forward as Gianfranco Zola got his marching orders (see pages 110–11). Job done – three reds in three games – the Mexican packed his cards and went home.

With four years to brood, Brizio Carter prepared for France '98 aiming to really make his mark. In front of 80,000 in Paris he took charge of the hosts' game against Saudi Arabia. He warmed up by flashing his red at Mohammed al-Khilaiwi for a trip after 17 minutes, but left his *pièce de résistance* until late in the second half, nailing the player of the tournament, Zinedine Zidane, whose stamp on Saudi captain Fuad Amin gave him – as they say – no option.

Now he had the taste for it and Arturo was saving his best for his biggest match ever: the quarter-final between Argentina and the Netherlands. It took ace red-card provocateur Diego Simeone (see page 29) to draw a cynical foul from the already cautioned Arthur Numan – a few rolls in agony and, presto, there was Brizio Carter with his arm raised. But the Mexican wasn't finished yet …

With the game entering the last couple of minutes at 1-1, Daniel Ortega (who had inherited Maradona's No. 10 shirt) rushed into the Dutch area. Theatrically plunging to the ground he appealed for a penalty. All eyes were on Arturo – could he resist a dismissal? Had defender Jaap Stam taken the Argentine out? Brizio Carter went to his pocket – only to produce a yellow for the dive. Surely he had missed his big chance? Events unfolded slowly, but the ref's dream soon came true. As Edwin van der Sar stood over Ortega, bawling him out, the midfielder rose and delivered a perfectly executed head-butt to the keeper's bonce. Arturo had his show-stopping moment after all.

Brizio Carter's World Cup ended there – leaving him with a record of seven red cards in six games and not one that anyone could really take issue with. There was, of course, one match in which he failed to deliver at France 98 – England v. Colombia. Shame, because with Ince, Scholes and Batty all on the pitch, you'd have thought they might have helped him out.

BILIC DRAWS A BLANC

France v. Croatia
World Cup, semi-final, Paris, 1998

The Croatian manager and chain-smoking rock guitarist Slaven Bilic, possesses a cool credibility that eludes virtually everyone else in football. Everyone loves Slaven Bilic these days. With the possible exception of Laurent Blanc …

It had been a memorable semi-final. Davor Suker scared the hosts by putting Croatia into the lead moments after half-time, but an unlikely brace from full-back Lilian Thuram had turned the fixture on its head. We were poised for a tense last 15 minutes as Zinedine Zidane whipped a free-kick into the Croatian area. With the ball still in the air, referee Jose Maria Garcia Aranda halted the game.

It seemed to be one of those pedantic interruptions refs like to make to draw attention to themselves – but for one player it was to have a devastating effect.

A pretty innocuous scuffle on the penalty spot between Blanc and Bilic had left the Croat on his knees clutching his forehead. It seemed the kind of spat that happens every time there's a crowd in the box, but the referee had no doubts. Blanc had to go. Ten-man France would hold on to make the final, but without the man they called 'Le President'.

Television replays revealed both players to have a good handful of the other's shirt and Blanc handing off his opponent with an open palm and brushing him on the chin. There was nothing to suggest Blanc had laid out his opponent. As usual, FIFA refused to reverse the decision. It would remain the only red card of Blanc's career and deny him the opportunity to play in the world's biggest match. His loss was Frank Leboeuf's gain – but even without their star defender, the French still managed to beat Brazil in the final.

Bilic remains unrepentant. 'I have not changed my version [of events],' he told *Le Parisien*. 'As on all corners, I was marking Laurent Blanc. Nothing had happened between us during the whole game. Then, out of nowhere, he hit me. It wasn't like Mike Tyson, but I was struck. I'm sorry that Laurent missed the final, genuinely, but the one to blame is him.'

'This time,' thinks Laurent Blanc. 'I really am going to deck him.'

And when the two met as respective national team managers in the Euro 2012 qualifiers, Blanc was happy to let bygones be viewed on YouTube. The French boss conceded all too reasonably, 'It's in the past. He says it was my fault and he was right.'

WORLD CUP STATISTICS

Total World Cup dismissals
11: Brazil
10: Argentina
8: Uruguay
7: Cameroon, Italy, Netherlands, (West) Germany
6: Mexico, Czechoslovakia/Czech Republic, France
5: Hungary, Yugoslavia/Serbia, Portugal
4: United States, Australia
3: Soviet Union, Denmark, Bulgaria, Croatia, Sweden, England, Chile
2: Bolivia, Belgium, Paraguay, Turkey, South Korea, Algeria, South Africa
1: Romania, Austria, Spain, Peru, United Arab Emirates, Honduras, Northern Ireland, Canada, Iraq, Scotland, Saudi Arabia, China, Senegal, Slovenia, Jamaica, Zaïre, Ghana, Tunisia, Ukraine, Angola, Poland, Togo, Trinidad & Tobago, Côte d'Ivoire, Switzerland, Nigeria

Total dismissals per tournament
1930: Uruguay, 1
1934: Italy, 1
1938: France, 4
1950: Brazil, 0
1954: Switzerland, 3
1958: Sweden, 3
1962: Chile, 6
1966: England, 5
1970: Mexico, 0
1974: West Germany, 5
1978: Argentina, 3
1982: Spain, 5

1986: Mexico, 8
1990: Italy, 16
1994: United States, 15
1998: France, 22
2002: Korea/Japan, 17
2006: Germany, 28
2010: South Africa, 17
Total: 159

Most dismissals in one match

4: Portugal v. Netherlands, 2006
(Costinha, Deco; Boulahrouz, Van Bronckhorst)

'Well, I think that seems to have calmed things down ...'

Most dismissals for one nation in a tournament

3: Argentina, 1990 (Giusti, Monzon, Dezotti)
France, 1998 (Zidane, Blanc, Desailly)
Cameroon, 1998 (Kalla, Song, Etame)

First dismissal
Plácido Galindo: Peru v. Romania, Uruguay 1930 (see page 113)

First red card
The red and yellow card system was not introduced until the 1970 World Cup. The first player to receive a red card was Chile's Carlos Caszely in 1974 in the 67th minute of their group match against West Germany.

First goalkeeper dismissed
Gianluca Pagliuca: Italy v. Norway, USA 1994

Fastest dismissal
56 seconds: Sergio Batista, Uruguay v. Scotland, 1986 (see pages 115–7)

Most dismissals
2: Zinedine Zidane, France v. Saudi Arabia, 1998
and France v. Italy, 2006
Rigobert Song, Cameroon v. Brazil, 1994
and Cameroon v. Chile, 1998

Sent off in final
Pedro Monzon and **Gustavo Abel Dezotti:** Argentina v. West Germany, 1990
Marcel Desailly: France v. Brazil, 1998
Zinedine Zidane: France v. Italy, 2006
Johnny Heitinga: Netherlands v. Spain, 2010

YOU DID WHAT?

→ • • • • • • • • • • • • • • •

You often hear the experts on TV or radio talking about players getting 'the red mist' or 'a rush of blood to the head' in an attempt to explain a random act of red card stupidity. But there are some moments when referees and players step into the arena of the ridiculous. These are the moments the fans really cherish …

11

▦ A COCK AND BALL STORY

The unfortunate ball in the groin. It brings a guaranteed giggle from 21 players and prolonged agony for one poor fellow. But for Aaron Eccleston in Melbourne, Australia, it brought more than a deep-rooted pain and a dull ache ...

Old Hill Wanderers were taking on Swinburne University Reserves as Aaron went up for a header, mistimed his jump and saw the ball make a direct hit on his meat and two veg. As he collapsed to the ground in considerable pain, the referee became aware that Aaron had an intimate body piercing. He was allowed to leave the field to get some attention and remove his body ring.

As he ran back on to the field, the referee demanded that Aaron proved he had removed the 'jewellery'; Aaron refused to show him. The referee then added insult to injury and proceeded to dish out two successive yellow cards to the still-suffering player: the first for re-entering the field of play without the referee's permission, and the second for refusing to prove that he had removed the piercing.

Eccleston, a 'disillusioned Mansfield Town fan, down under' according to his Twitter page, was shocked at how quickly the story spread, tweeting, 'I don't think my mum's going to be particularly happy!'

▦ WHEN PUSH COMES TO SHOVE

Paolo Di Canio
Sheffield Wednesday v. Arsenal, Hillsborough, 1998

What do you need to do to get a £10,000 fine and an 11-match ban? A wild two-footed challenge? Break an opponent's jaw with a haymaker? How about a gentle push to the flabby tummy of a wibbly, wobbly referee? Because that's what did for Paolo Di Canio when Sheffield Wednesday met Arsenal in a Premier League match in September 1998.

Di Canio had already been shown the red for a spat with Patrick Vieira, but was incensed that Martin Keown's aggressive reaction had, so far, gone uncensored. As the Italian delivered a theatrical but non-violent push ('I could have pushed my eight-year-old daughter

Ludovica that way and she wouldn't have fallen over,' he later claimed), referee Paul Alcock stumbled backwards and eventually fell on his arse.

The whole incident was made hilarious by the ref's ungainly stagger, worthy of a circus clown, but was followed by an equally amusing postscript. As Di Canio left the pitch, Nigel Winterburn raced across to pile salt on the wound, informing the Italian that he'd gone too far and that his career was over. As Di Canio paused to look at the workaday full-back, Winterburn performed his own pantomime act – flinching dramatically, rearing away like a frightened child and finding a convenient divot to replace.

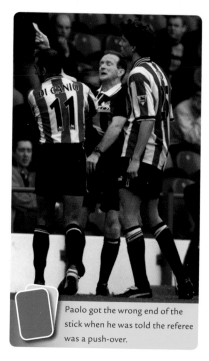

Paolo got the wrong end of the stick when he was told the referee was a push-over.

Di Canio's career at Hillsborough was indeed over, but he would soon reinvent himself as a West Ham hero and FIFA saint: winning their Fair Play Award in 2001 for catching a cross he was about to convert until he saw Everton keeper Paul Gerrard grounded by an injury. By January 2012 he was manager of Swindon Town and back in trouble, sent to the stands this time for kicking one of his players up the arse, as his team played Macclesfield Town.

▦ HE'S GOT A GOOD ENGINE ...

With the exception of goody-two-shoes Gary Lineker, everyone gets their marching orders sooner or later. But it's a matter of how you respond that counts. Take Joseph Rimmer. He was playing for Lonsdale against Southport and District League rivals Harrington in February 2010, when referee David Harkness ignored his appeals for a foul. His abuse of the man in black soon led to the ref reaching for his pocket. But before Harkness could take hold of the red, Rimmer was threatening him, saying, 'If you book me or send me off you know what will happen.'

The ref didn't know. Indeed who might have guessed? Maybe the player on the next pitch who was surprised to see Rimmer trudging through the middle of their game muttering: 'Watch me run the f****** ref over.' Still fuming, he got into his Range Rover, drove across both pitches and headed for the ref. As Harkness hid in the goal, 28-year-old Rimmer did 'donuts', spinning his 4x4 around in 360-degree circles, before getting out, making a playground gun of his fingers and announcing his intention to shoot the terrified official.

In Liverpool Crown Court, Rimmer claimed he was just trying to get the match abandoned. He received a 24-week jail sentence.

▦ DANGEROUS WHEN CORNERED

Former Stoke City, West Brom, Fulham and endless Division One teams' striker Paul Peschisolido was sent off for using the corner flag as a weapon when playing for Canada against El Salvador in a World Cup qualifier in 1997. In his defence, Peschisolido claimed he had actually been trying to elbow the player, but missed and elbowed the flag into his face instead – oh, that's OK then ...

▦ NOW THAT'S WHAT I CALL DISSENT!

February 2008, Thailand. Kuiburi FC were up against Kasem Bundit at the stadium in Ayutthaya, north of Bangkok, in a play-off to decide promotion to the country's second division. With Kasem Bundit leading, referee Prakong Sukguamala sent off three of the Kuiburi players, putting the rest of the team into a rare old paddy.

In the ensuing mayhem the ref, quite sensibly, beat a retreat to his dressing room, but was followed in by the still-angry players who began to administer a beating to the poor official. Police firing gunshots into the air managed to disperse the players, but they then chased Prakong into the stadium's office. Safe at last, he locked himself in – and promptly walked straight into a mirror.

The referee needed 50 stitches, admittedly some due to cuts from the broken mirror, and he also broke a finger, while the Football Association of Thailand handed down life bans to seven Kuiburi players.

THE MASK OF SORROW

By the time you read this, Brazilian wunderkind Neymar may well be plying his trade at Chelsea, Man City, Barcelona or Barnet (OK, maybe not there), but back in April 2011 he was still wooing admirers with his displays for São Paulo's Santos. His winning effort in a 3-2 victory over Chile's Colo Colo in the Copa Libertadores was particularly memorable – for the execution and the consequences.

The then 19-year-old, who had already scored three goals in three games for his national team, took a mazy run, flicking the ball past two Colo Colo defenders before chipping the keeper to put Santos ahead in the 52nd minute.

Neymar's celebration – not quite as cool as he thinks!

Running in celebration to the touchline, he took one of the thousands of paper Neymar masks worn by the crowd and put it on. Now, as you are no doubt aware, strutting around wearing your own face on a bit of paper attached by an elastic band is a breach of one of FIFA's myriad rules, so Uruguayan referee Roberto Carlos Silvera brandished the prodigy's second yellow, and sent him on his way.

▦ TAKE THAT AND DEPART-Y

Robbie Williams, yes he of Take That and numerous number one hits, was born above a pub, a mere two minutes walk from Vale Park stadium, home to Burslem's Port Vale. Not for him, the prawn sandwiches and executive boxes of Old Trafford, and to his credit, throughout his celebrity days Robbie has always remained a Valiant.

The singer was therefore pretty chuffed to be asked to strut his stuff in front of the Vale thousands (OK, hundreds) when invited to play in Dean Glover's testimonial against Aston Villa in 1998. At the peak of his popularity as a solo star, Robbie donned the team's famous white shirt and looked by no means out of place among his heroes.

After confidently slotting away a penalty, Robbie's over-the-top celebrations included dishing out the verbals to the referee. If he thought he was too famous to see red, Robbie was mistaken – with a great display of disbelief and frustration, he was forced to take the walk of shame. Dismissed on his only ever appearance in Vale's colours.

Glover himself later told the *Independent*, it was actually a case of Robbie once again playing the showman, 'It was all planned because he needed a quick getaway. It was probably the only sending-off ever when the player actually wanted to go.' Oh well, as the man himself sang, 'Let me entertain you' ... (at least until the red card appears).

▦ WHEN TEAMMATES ATTACK

It's good enough to watch when an opposition player sees red, but even better when it's the result of a little fisticuffs between teammates. And, if you get both taking the long walk – bonanza! Of course, in the professional game such incidents are pretty rare, but that's why we need to savour the great ones ...

Derek Hales v. Mike Flanagan
Charlton Athletic, 1979

Like Peters and Lee, and Mike and Bernie Winters, Hales and Flanagan were one of those great 1970s partnerships that had started to flag as the 1980s drew near. That said though, they set the bar for same-team scrapping as Charlton played out an FA Cup draw with local neighbours non-league Maidstone.

When Flanagan, having put Hales through on goal, whined at his strike partner for straying offside, the permed duo set about each other, both eventually taking the early bath. Hales, who threw the first punch, was sacked instantly by the club, but Flanagan suffered a worse fate – he was sold to Crystal Palace. Hales was back a month later, reinstated after a legal challenge, and was eventually made captain.

Five years later, Flanagan found his way back to The Valley to re-join his sparring partner. Hales was clearly peeved and after a few column inches were filled with his fuming, he was forced to give up the armband and write his name on the transfer list.

Lee Bowyer v. Kieron Dyer
Newcastle United, 2005

The two midfielders faced up to each other over Dyer's passing ability after the Magpies had fallen three behind at home to Aston Villa. Dyer went for the Greco-Roman style, ripping a chunk out of Bowyer's collar, while Lee was more of a bar-room brawler, throwing punches 10 to the dozen. Villa's Gareth Barry played peacemaker and then off the duo trawled – reappearing at a press conference later sitting either side of boss Graeme Souness, and looking like schoolboys in detention.

Bowyer pleaded guilty to using threatening behaviour at a Newcastle Magistrates' Court, confessing he ignited the scrap because Dyer did not pass him the ball. The court fined Bowyer £600, the FA banned him for three games and fined him £30,000. The club then fined Bowyer six weeks' wages. Amazingly he bore no grudge, two years later welcoming Kieron Dyer alongside him at West Ham.

Craig Levein v. Graeme Hogg
Hearts, 2004
Pre-season friendlies are all about bonding, getting a better understanding of your teammates and gelling as an outfit. Hearts' run-out against Raith Rovers didn't exactly work out like that when Craig Levein laid out his fellow defender Graeme Hogg with some style. Levein, now coach of the Scottish national team, didn't take kindly to a little constructive criticism from Hoggy and went medieval on his so-called mate.

Hogg, a six-footer who turned out for Man Utd in the mid-1980s, was no match for the usually mild-mannered Levein. He had his nose broken and, by the time the ref was waving a red at both of them, he was sparko on a stretcher. 'I didn't see the punch coming,' Hogg admitted later. 'And I didn't see the red card, either.'

Ricardo Fuller v. Andy Griffin
Stoke City, 2008
At Upton Park, Stoke City's Ricardo Fuller took the taboo a step further. It's one thing to belt a teammate, but quite another to manhandle your skipper. Fuller delivered a slap to Andy Griffith after his captain had botched a clearance and given away a goal. 'I said to Griff, "clear the ball out" and he was rude and disrespectful,' Fuller told the BBC. As Stoke prepared to kick off, the two came together in the centre circle and Fuller did enough to get the referee reaching for his red. There are not many recipients of the red card who walk off hearing their own captain telling them exactly where to go.

▦ AIN'T NOBODY HERE BUT US CHICKENS!

Like a charming good-looking and wealthy boyfriend, we all think he's the one – only for him to up sticks, leaving us heartbroken and looking foolish. But once upon a time Carlos Tevez was a one-club player. Scratch Carlos and you'll discover Buenos Aires' Boca Juniors are still his team – and their bonkers supporters have reason to keep a special place for him in their hearts.

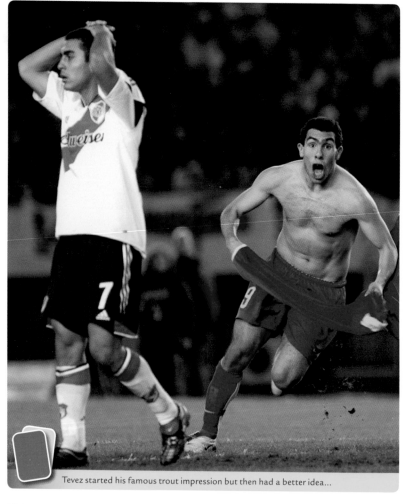

Tevez started his famous trout impression but then had a better idea...

They truly bonded in a 2004 Copa Libertadores semi-final tie between Boca and their bitter rivals River Plate – a confrontation the *Observer* said made the Old Firm derby look like 'a primary school kickabout'. While River Plate fans make a big thing of the stench of the industrial setting of their neighbours' Bombonera Stadium, Los Bosteros (the manure handlers) hark back to 1966 to mock their hated rivals' shock Intercontinental Cup defeat to Penarol by calling River Plate, 'The Chickens'.

Got all that? Right, back to 2004. It's the 85th minute and River Plate lead 1-0. Boca break and Tevez sweeps in an equaliser. In front of the stunned and silent home fans, 'El Apache' goes berserk, whipping his shirt off and performing Boca fans' famous chicken dance. For a moment it looked like referee Hector Baldassi was joining in the fun, but it became apparent his dance was just a way of explaining why Tevez was being shown the red. Still, Carlos had the last laugh – Boca went on to win on penalties.

▦ 'UNBELIEVABLE JEFF!'

Portsmouth v. Blackburn
Soccer Saturday, **Sky TV, April 2010**

Jeff Stelling: 'And now off to Fratton Park where there's been a red card. But for who? Chris Kamara ...'

Chris Kamara: 'I don't know. Has there? [turns to face pitch then looks back at camera] I must have missed that. Red card? [shrugs and looks back at the pitch].'

Jeff Stelling: 'According to our sources Anthony van den Borre has been sent off. Get your fingers out and count the number of Portsmouth players on the field.'

Chris Kamara: 'No, you're right. I saw him go off, but I thought they were bringing a sub on.'

Cue mass hysterics in Sky TV studio ...

▦ GOD'S OTHER HAND

Uruguay v. Ghana

World Cup, quarter-final, Johannesburg, South Africa, 2010

'The Hand of God now belongs to me ...' said Luis Suarez. 'I made the best save of the tournament.' In the dying seconds of extra-time during Uruguay's quarter-final against Ghana, the forward had instinctively – and literally – taken destiny into his own hands, and helped take his team to the World Cup semi-finals.

With the score at 1-1, penalties looked inevitable, but Ghana had one last chance – a free-kick on the right wing, 10 yards outside their opponents' penalty area. It was one final opportunity to win a game that had been a tense struggle, but the most compelling match of the tournament.

Every youngster should study his stance, hand position – and complete lack of sportsmanship.

As the free-kick arced into the area, Ghana's Boateng got an early flick, Mensah knocked it back into the six-yard box and Owusu-Abeyie hooked it goalwards. The ball flew back off the knee of goal-line-stationed Suarez, but Adiyiah was the first to react with a bullet header. Defender Fucile, leaping to head it clear, was inches short, but just behind him was Suarez – with no time to jump he simply punched the ball away.

As the red card was raised, Suarez left the field in tears. The Ghanaians tried not to over-celebrate, but smiles and glances betrayed their belief that the game was won. Asamoah Gyan, who had already converted two spot-kicks in the tournament, stood on the verge of taking an African team to the last four of the World Cup for the first time. His strike initially looked good, but it had pace and was rising fast. Skimming the crossbar, it flew up and into the stand behind the goal. Suarez's tears dried up in an instant as he punched his fists in pure delight.

Ghana will lose the shoot-out now, said sofa-psychologists around the world – and they were right. Mensah and Adiyiah missed their penalties and the devil had triumphed: Uruguay were through and Suarez was carried shoulder high as the hero of the hour, his unashamed celebrations leaving a bitter taste for many around the world.

As self-sacrifices go, the gifted striker had perhaps taken the greatest red card ever, one that could ultimately have seen his team make the World Cup final – a match for which he would probably be have been suspended. Unfortunately, without him, Uruguay didn't make it past the Netherlands and Suarez is just remembered for being a desperate cheat with a lack of humility...

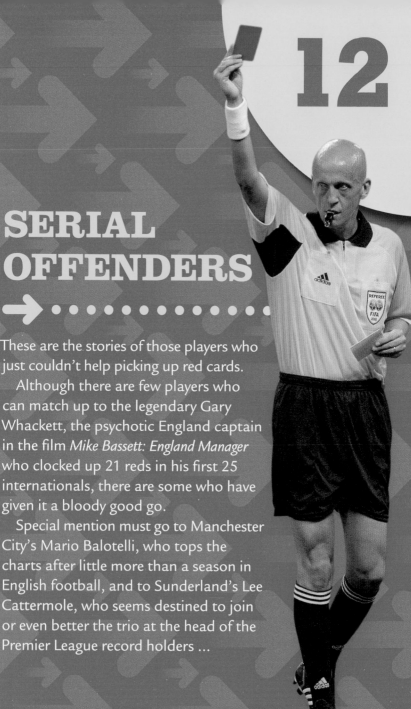

SERIAL
OFFENDERS

→ • • • • • • • • • • • • • •

These are the stories of those players who just couldn't help picking up red cards.

Although there are few players who can match up to the legendary Gary Whackett, the psychotic England captain in the film *Mike Bassett: England Manager* who clocked up 21 reds in his first 25 internationals, there are some who have given it a bloody good go.

Special mention must go to Manchester City's Mario Balotelli, who tops the charts after little more than a season in English football, and to Sunderland's Lee Cattermole, who seems destined to join or even better the trio at the head of the Premier League record holders ...

PREMIER LEAGUE RED CARDS PER GAMES PLAYED (MINIMUM 3 REDS)

Mario Balotelli: played 40 games/3 reds = one red every 13.33 matches

Duncan Ferguson: played 186 games/8 reds = one red every 23.25 matches

John Hartson: played 141 games/6 reds = one red every 23.5 matches

Alex Rae: played 102 games/4 reds = one red every 25.5 matches

Nikos Dabizas: played 137 games/5 reds = one red every 27.4 matches

Lee Cattermole: played 140 games/6 reds = one red every 28.33 matches

Vinnie Jones: played 178 games/6 reds = one red every 29.7 matches

Patrick Vieira: played 284 games/8 reds = one red every 35.5 matches

Jason Roberts: played 142 games/4 reds = one red every 35.5 matches

Kerimoglu Tugay: played 183 games/5 reds = one red every 36.6 matches

C'EST CHIC …

'How come I was ordered off so many times in my career? I reckon it's because I kept getting caught.' Chic Charnley was sent off 17 times in all, one of which, he claims in an autobiography called *Seeing Red*, was a complete injustice.

James 'Chic' Charnley was a hard-living Glaswegian whose sweet left foot might have won him a place in the Scotland squad if it wasn't for his penchant for getting his retaliation in first. The Ayr, Partick, St Mirren, Dundee … (carry on listing every non-Old Firm side north of the border) player still dines out on the story of how he chased off samurai sword-wielding critics while training, but his on-field antics weren't quite so heroic. Late tackles, off-the-ball incidents, revenge attacks – Chic broke just about every rule in the book and paid the price.

His wall of shame includes: ambushing Dundee United's Darren Jackson in the tunnel, spitting at an Ayr player, decking his own teammate in his last game for Dundee and signing for Clydebank despite being dismissed in both his trials. In his last game for Ayr, a reserve match at Ibrox, he was sent off for a late challenge, and left the pitch flicking the Vs at the fans and ostentatiously blessing himself!

Referee Wally Young, who was responsible for four of his red cards, described Charnley as 'wired to the moon'. Wally was the ref at Henrik Larsson's Celtic debut against Chic's Hibs when Charnley's daughter was the mascot. At the coin toss she asked Wally not to send her daddy off today. 'Who's your daddy?' asked Scotland's leading official with a smile. When she pointed at Charnley, he could only reply, 'I can't promise'. Still, the old softie let him off with a booking on that occasion.

▦ WHO'S THE DADDY?

So who's really the daddy of the Premier League wrong 'uns? It has to be 'Duncan Disorderly', the man who was sent, not just off, but to the notorious Barlinnie Prison in Glasgow for his footballing crimes.

Ferguson could be devastating, but you never knew whether you'd be taken apart by a bullet header or a Glasgow kiss. He was a throwback to another era: a bristling, bruising barn door of a forward, but Big Dunc could play too, notching 100 goals – many of them superbly executed headers – in a career that took him from Dundee United to Rangers and on to Newcastle and Everton.

Amazingly, Ferguson escaped even a yellow for the headbutt to Raith's John McStay that led to his prison sentence, but the crimson curse was never far away from the man from Stirling. He became used to bathing alone thanks to the flying elbows that floored Paolo Wanchope, Hermann Hreidarsson and Kostas Konstantinidis, his attempt to strangle Leicester's Steffen Freund after receiving his second yellow, or the cussing that persuaded David Elleray to book him twice for dissent in the last minute of a game.

In January 2006, Dunc walked for the last time, laying out Paul Scharner with a punch to the solar plexus that nearly ripped through

'That wasn't a headbutt ref, *this* is a headbutt.'

the Austrian's stomach. Later the Wigan defender was almost reverential, 'He got sent off, but I began to appreciate how he earned his reputation as a hardman. It was a nice punch, I have to say.'

DENNIS THE MENACE

The Birmingham City team of the 1980s was a walking *Who's Who* of footballing hardmen. Their ranks numbered Robert Hopkins, Pat van den Hauwe and Mick Harford, but there were few as scary as Mark 'The Menace' Dennis. An assured left-back who also became cult hero at Southampton and QPR, Dennis was considered good enough to have challenged Kenny Sansom's England position – if he hadn't had a knack of leaving wingers writhing on the ground.

Mark, who earned the nickname 'Psycho' when Stuart Pearce was still cleaning Brian Clough's car, was one of the few players his own trade union has considered expelling. He had already been sent off 10 times by the time he'd reached the age of 26. In 1987, his elbow on Ossie Ardiles' face delivered the 11th card of his career and led to an eight-game ban. QPR chairman David Bulstrode wrote to the FA vowing to terminate his contract if he stepped out of line again. A year later, he was dismissed again after spitting at a Fulham player in a reserve game. By that time Bulstrode had sadly passed on, but Dennis was soon shipped out to Crystal Palace to see out his career.

COMES WITH AN 18 CERTIFICATE

Tomas Repka – you've got to hand it to the guy, he's consistent. The Czech hardman has picked up 18 red cards over his career, managing at least one for every club he played for (with the exception of his latest club České Budějovice – at the time of writing), including the Czech Under-21s, for whom he made only two appearances, and the full national team.

Hard-tackling, quick-tempered, aggressive and well ... a little mad, Tomas didn't seem to care how he got his early bath. He missed out on the Euros in 1996, when the Czech Republic reached the final, after taking our Spain's Raul in an Under-21 match. He moved on to Italian side Fiorentina for whom he managed to amass five red cards in 87 appearances (one every 17 games) between 1998 and 2001.

So West Ham knew what they were getting when they signed him for £5.5 million in 2001 – a cultured international defender with some minor anger management problems. He didn't let them down. In his debut at Middlesbrough he made it through to half-time without exercising the ref's writing hand, but two late tackles in the second half earned a yellow each, and we know what that means. In just his third game he was off again, getting the double yellow once more as the Hammers went down 7-1 to Blackburn. Super Tom was off on the road to cult status down Essex way.

A few weeks later, he made it three in nine matches when he headbutted Belgium's Bart Goor shortly before the break in the Czech Republic's World Cup play-off in Prague. As his nation failed to make the finals, Tomas was the scapegoat. 'I just can't change. I do not want to hurt the team but I'll always be the same,' the defender told newspaper *Mlada Fronta Dnes* after the match. He would never again appear for his country.

He left West Ham a legend in 2006, having notched up four dismissals in five years, to return to Sparta Prague and exercise refs' writing hands in his homeland once again. In a league match against FC Teplice, billed as a tribute to the opponents' coach who had died earlier that week, Repka was shown a second yellow for abusing the Teplice staff. On the way to the tunnel, Tom took exception to being followed by a cameraman, punching the camera and sending the cameraman sprawling.

Less than a year later, he'd mastered getting sent off to such an extent that he managed to get dismissed for throwing the ball at an FC Brno player's face – in the very first minute of the match.

▦ 'THE MOST HATED MAN IN FOOTBALL'

It's 1996, and as Norwich City take on Crystal Palace a young defender recently signed from South Melbourne body-checks City's Darren Eadie. In the midst of the subsequent ugly brawl, he is the first to be dismissed. British football had met Kevin Muscat – and he would make sure it would never forget him.

When elbows and headbutts failed, Muscat would use the deathly Spock grip.

Over the next nine seasons Muscat would notch up 12 red cards, and not softy, dissent or shirt-tugging ones either – many of them were for vicious challenges or angry assaults. At Palace, Wolves, Rangers (where he wasn't risked in Old Firm matches) and Millwall, Muscat built a scary reputation, which peaked when Birmingham City's Martin Grainger called him 'the most hated man in football'.

His list of convictions include: walking after just nine minutes at Grimsby for elbowing a player in the face, being threatened with the sack after three weeks at Millwall following a stamp on Watford's Danny Webber and receiving a five-game suspension for clattering Sheffield United's Ashley Ward from behind and igniting a mass brawl. Shortly after his 12th red, for headbutting Sheffield United's Paddy Kenny in a tunnel bust-up, Muscat returned to Australia.

At Melbourne Victory he carried on as he left off – off-the-ball assaults, flying elbows, dangerous tackles – even managing a new feat of back-to-back red cards. In all he was dismissed a further five times. The last came in January 2011 after he had just served a suspension for elbowing Adelaide United midfielder Adam Hughes in the face. Returning for the Melbourne derby, Muscat committed a horror challenge on Melbourne Heart's Adrian Zahra, described by the *Sun* as one of the worst tackles in football history. He received an eight-match ban and universal condemnation.

Muscat, capped over 50 times for his country, was rated and liked by many in the game, but many more breathed a sigh of relief when he hung up the boots that had left stud marks on players' legs, ankles and feet in leagues on either side of the world.

▦ TELL 'EM ABOUT THE HONEY MONSTER

When Richard Dunne kicked out at Amr Zaki in the closing stages of Manchester City's 1-0 win over Wigan Athletic in January 2009, he joined a select group of Premier League bad boys: he had equalled Patrick Vieira and Duncan Ferguson's record of eight red cards in the league. But for once those clichéd words rang true – 'he's not that kind of player'.

Dunne's nickname isn't 'Psycho', 'Meathead' or 'The Terminator'. Nope, he goes under the moniker of the 'Honey Monster', an affectionate reference to the lovable if stupid character from 1970s Sugar Puff adverts. That's because the dependable Everton, Manchester City, Aston Villa and Republic of Ireland defender is no wild tackler or fly-off-the-handle merchant. Most of his dismissals come from his desperate, last-ditch, if sometimes clumsy efforts to save the day – it's no coincidence that Dunne also holds the record for the most ever own-goals in the Premier League.

The Honey Monster has racked up his cards in over 400 league games since his debut in 1997, and includes in his collection a dismissal in the FA and UEFA Cups, and red cards for the Under-21 and full Republic of Ireland sides.

Though loved by fans for his wholehearted efforts (he won Manchester City's Player of the Year award for four successive seasons), Dunne's reds do mark him out as a scapegoat. A straight red after quarter of an hour led to an 8-1 thrashing at Middlesbrough in May 1998, and the defender got more than his fair share of the blame for City's exit from the quarter-finals of the UEFA Cup after picking up a second yellow against Hamburg a year later.

As the only one of the leaders still playing, there is still hope that the Villa defender can become the Premier League's outright red card king. Come on Honey Monster! Just one more mistimed lunge and you're there ...

ROY MCDONOUGH

If there is a time to use the phrase 'More cards than Clintons', it's now. Roy 'Doughnut' McDonough is said to have amassed 21 red ones in an 18-year career in the non and lower leagues, but the 13 league dismissals the striker and occasional centre-half earned during his spells with Walsall (one), Exeter City (two), Colchester United (three) and Southend United (seven) between 1978 and 1994 will do for now.

In his book, *England's Worst Footballers*, Sky Sports TV presenter Jeff Stelling nominated McDonough as Colchester's worst ever player, saying, 'The red mist occasionally descends on some players and Roy McDonough spent his whole career in a disciplinary pea-souper.' Although a little unfair on a player who was a free-scoring hero at Colchester and Southend, his mixture of a fondness for the physical side of the game and an ability to lose his head in an instant did get the better of him a little too often.

Red Card Roy eventually became player-manager at Colchester and succeeded in returning the Layer Road club to the Football League. He celebrated by getting sent off twice in their first season back.

▥ MEET MR MAD …

'Lehmann is the Mr Mad of the goalkeeper society,' Brian Woolnough wrote in the *Daily Star*. He was being polite. Jens is as bonkers as a bag of fish. And, though we saw his eccentricities in his days as Arsenal's custodian, he saved his biggest slices of fruitcake for his time in Germany, collecting the record for most red cards for any Borussia Dortmund player as well as for any goalkeeper in the German Bundesliga.

He first went in April 1999, but since then he's added another four more reds to his famous Champions League exit with Arsenal (see pages 45–6). Of course, Jens's indiscretions aren't just last line of defence fouls – they include pulling an opponent's hair in the final minute of a league game and charging out of his goal to shove teammate Marcio Amorose. 'There is no rule that the goalkeeper must not run out of the penalty area,' Lehmann later said. 'They must have invented that today.'

He saved his best for last. Stuttgart were leading Mainz 1-0 with three minutes to go. It would be their first Bundesliga victory for over two months. The now 40-year-old Lehmann gathered the ball safely, but for reasons known only to him, stamped viciously on the Mainz striker Aristide Bancé's foot. Bancé hit the deck, the ref pointed to the spot, off went Mad Jens and Mainz claimed the draw.

Rushing from the ground as quickly as possible, Lehmann found himself mingling with the disgruntled exiting fans, but one Stuttgart fan took up the matter of the keeper's match-chucking antics. Instead of replying, Lehmann snatched the fan's glasses and walked off with them – only to return with them a minute later and hand them back. Barking, utterly, utterly barking ...

THANK GOD IT'S NOT FRIDAY

The George Best of the lower leagues, Reading and Cardiff City striker Robin Friday was supremely talented but unreliable, rebellious, fond of a drink – and constantly on the verge of savouring the ref's armpit odour.

Robin Friday, presumably celebrating his second goal.

By the end of his time at amateur level, playing for Walthamstow Avenue and Hayes, Friday had been sent off seven times in three years and in 1975 he became the first Reading player to be dismissed in nearly eight years. He once told the *South Wales Echo*, 'On the pitch I hate all opponents. I don't give a damn about anyone. People think I'm mad, a lunatic. I am a winner.'

Despite dying aged 39 in 1990, the wild-living Friday's career is full of great, if unsubstantiated, stories such as the time he leaped the advertising boards to take a nip from a spectator's whisky bottle. Jumping back onto the pitch, he was promptly booked for leaving without permission. He supposedly protested, saying, 'But, ref, I haven't had my pint chaser yet,' and received a red card in reply.

Another story surrounds Friday's dismissal at Brighton in 1977 in his last ever game for Cardiff. Having been hounded all day by Mark Lawrenson, the striker drew the moustachioed defender into a slide tackle and left his foot in his face. That much we know. The no-doubt apocryphal story has it that the expelled Friday broke into the opposition's dressing room and took a dump in Lawrenson's kit bag. Remember that image next time he bores you on *Match of the Day*!

STEVE WALSH

What kind of liability do you have to be to get moved up front because you can't be trusted not to get sent off? Leicester City's Steve Walsh was an old-fashioned, heart-on-his-sleeve, 'orrible, bruisin' centre-back – the kind of whom 'Arry Redknapp would say, 'You'd want him on your team, wouldn't ya?' But after Leicester's heroic defender had picked up seven red cards between October 1986 and November 1992, boss Brian Little decided to move him out of trouble and play him as a striker. It was a masterstroke from the manager – Walsh was top scorer in the 1992-93 season with 15 goals. Nevertheless, he'd still manage to clock up a record-equalling 13 red cards by the end of his career.

▦ VINNIE JONES

Can you imagine Nobby Stiles in *The Godfather* or David Batty in *Reservoir Dogs*? Sounds ridiculous but while some play up to the hardman tag and others try their best to shake it off, Vinnie Jones is the only one to have made a Hollywood career of it.

Perhaps it's because Vinnie always seemed a cartoon character first and a footballer second that he bridged the gap so easily. After all, this is the man who grabbed Gazza's wotsits, got the fastest ever yellow card (in two seconds) and threatened to bite Kenny Dalglish's ear off and spit in the hole before an FA Cup final.

You know those flying two-footed challenges that everyone gets hot under the collar about these days? That was Vinnie's modus operandi. That, and a tendency to go off on one at the slightest opportunity, was what earned the self-confessed 'creator of havoc' a whopping 12 red cards. Vinnie, whose advice in his *Soccer's Hard Man* video was, 'If their top geezer gets sorted out early doors, you win', went for high-profile victims. He stuck the nut on Kevin Ratcliffe and Stan Collymore, flattened Graham Rix, punched Anders Limpar for not suffering enough from his studs-up challenge and clattered Ruud Gullit (before accusing foreigners of 'squealing like fat-bellied pigs'). Jones even managed to get sent off for Wales in one of only nine appearances.

Vinnie didn't discriminate though. In 1989, FA Cup-winners Wimbledon played a friendly against a village side in Shanklin, Isle of Wight. Tempers were a little frayed after some nightclub banter between the teams the night before and when someone had a go at Dennis Wise after a corner, Vinnie was first on the scene. Perhaps misunderstanding the nature of a friendly, Jones lumped a local milkman and received the most meaningless red of his career. Boss Bobby Gould was so fed up with his loose cannon that he made him sit on the bus alone, and miss out on the tea and homemade cakes provided by the locals after the match.

Vinnie has always claimed he could also play a bit – he certainly had a useful long throw – but he left his real epitaph in the wake of being fined for his abovementioned video: 'The FA have given me a pat on the back. I've taken violence off the terraces and on to the pitch.'

WILLIE JOHNSTON

Poor old Willie – or 'Bud' as he was often called. Scotland's fall guy in the 1978 World Cup finals tops the Bad Boy charts, but you can't help feeling a little sorry for him. Speedy, tricky wing play was his game, but 'retaliation' was his middle name and it would get him in a whole heap of trouble – 21 heaps in all.

Bud broke into the Rangers side in the mid-1960s, but by 1970 he had been sent off five times and banned for a total of 105 days. It was a dangerous time to be a ball player in Scotland and every single dismissal was a reaction to being hacked to pieces by an oafish full back. When he went south to West Brom in 1972, however, it seemed he'd picked up the habit for life – even extending his

Willie Johnston, a wee bit of trouble...

repertoire to attempting to boot the referee up the jacksy at Brighton in 1977.

In spells at Vancouver Whitecaps, back at Rangers and Hearts, Bud managed to enhance his collection. When the Whitecaps played the New York Cosmos, Johnston managed to incite a 20-man brawl (Alan Ball and Franz Beckenbauer sitting it out in the centre circle). His sparring partner, Cosmos' Giorgio Chinaglia, was also sent off and decided to follow Bud to the dressing room for a little afters. As things were about to get tasty, in walked Johnston's teammate John Craven, having seen red himself. Cue Chinaglia's hasty retreat to the Cosmos dressing room.

Back at Rangers, Willie courted controversy yet again. Sitting on the bench, he became obsessed with the physical approach being shown by Aberdeen's Willie Miller. When he was eventually sent on, Johnston made a beeline for Miller. He scythed him down and stamped on his throat. The player needed the kiss of life – but it wasn't Miller. Bud had got the wrong guy and nearly killed John McMaster.

Johnston's autobiography is called *Sent off at Gunpoint*, a title derived from a friendly Rangers played in New York against Fiorentina in June 1969. Bud had taken exception to being dismissed merely for questioning the parentage of an Italian defender, stood his ground and refused to go, but Bud wasn't accounting for the New York Police Department, whose gun-toting officer dug his weapon into the winger's ribs. The now terrified winger decided to walk. 'I had to go anyway,' he wrote. 'I needed the men's room.'

THE GREATEST EVER RED CARD

→ • • • • • • • • • • • • • •

What makes a great red card? I think we'd all agree on an element of violence and an element of theatre. But I'd suggest we also need a sense of occasion, a moment of high drama and the X-factor – something hilarious, surreal or completely off-the-wall. The truly great red card boasts a number of these. So, for what it's worth, here are my top five (in reverse order, of course):

5. Eric Cantona (page 65)
4. David Beckham (page 29)
3. Luis Suarez (page 138)
2. Billy Bremner/Kevin Keegan (page 46)

But there can really only be one contender for The Greatest Red Card Ever …

▦ A MAN'S GOTTA DO WHAT A MAN'S GOTTA DO

'I have nothing but contempt for Materazzi ... I want his balls on a platter,' Zidane's mother told the *Mirror*. A mother perhaps is not expected to forgive a vile insult to her daughter, but an experienced player, the best player in the world for a decade – surely he'd heard worse?

The 2006 World Cup final between France and Italy was set for a fairy-tale ending, with Zidane, already winner of the Golden Ball for best player of the tournament, destined to lift the famous trophy in his last ever football match.

France had taken the lead just seven minutes into the game with a penalty converted by their hero and, despite an equaliser by Marco Materazzi, Les Bleus seemed the more likely side to score in extra time. Zidane nearly secured the lead with a header that was tipped over by keeper Buffon, but that was to be his last meaningful action – on the ball.

The match had reached the 100th minute when Zidane and Materazzi came together at the edge of Italy's area. The former Everton defender lightly grabbed Zizou's shirt from behind, and after a few quiet words the matter seemed over. Suddenly, though, the French genius stopped in his tracks, turned back and delivered a firm headbutt to his opponent's upper chest. The blow was enough to knock Materazzi's six-foot-four frame straight to the ground.

The referee, Horatio Elizondo, hadn't seen the clash, but, once informed by his fourth official, had no alternative but to send Zidane packing. Without their talisman, France spluttered into penalties and without their spot-kick king they surrendered the trophy to the Italians. Ceremony over, people could concentrate on the real talking point: the red card.

Zizou was the best-loved player in the world. He was a footballing alchemist with exquisite balance and a wonderful touch, and had won every major trophy in the world. People struggled to equate this with such an ugly attack – surely he was responding to something worse? The rumours of racist abuse proved unfounded as both players revealed a similar story. Zidane had sarcastically told Marco he'd have to wait for the game to finish before getting his shirt. Materazzi took

offence at his haughtiness and flung the time-honoured continental mother-sister-whore insult. That was it. Zap! He'd hit the deck.
To this day the French star remains unrepentant, insisting he couldn't have lived with himself if he'd let the comment go.

In the end, the finale was more like a Western than a fairy tale. No smiles and celebrations, just a great player disappearing into the Berlin sunset – having done what he had to do ...

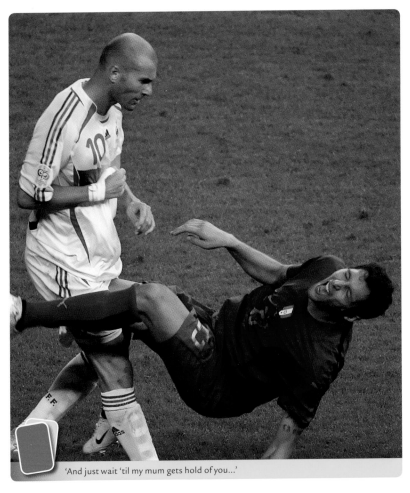

'And just wait 'til my mum gets hold of you...'

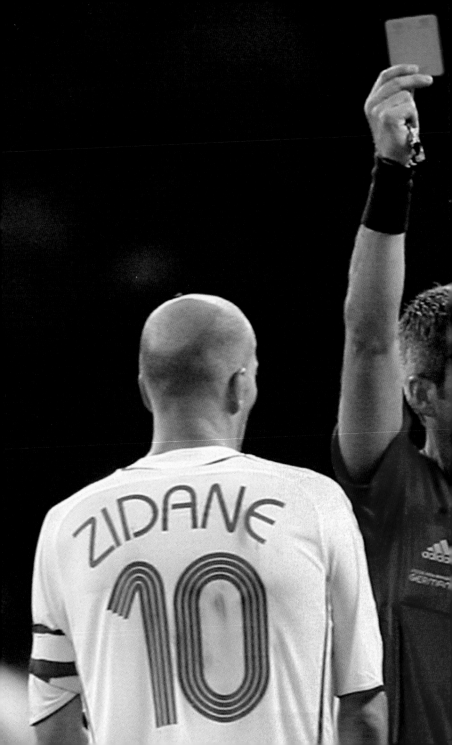

▦ ACKNOWLEDGEMENTS AND PICTURE CREDITS

Acknowledgements

This book would never have seen the light of day without the encouragement and enthusiasm of Ian Marshall, Craig Stevens and Julian Flanders (who also applied his expert editing skills to my words).

I would also like to acknowledge the help and suggestions of many friends, especially Julian Lewis, whose marvellous Tommy Gemmell-style red card (see page 100) on a windswept East London astroturf pitch remains the greatest dismissal I have witnessed first-hand.

Picture credits

The Publishers would like to thank the following for providing copyright photographs included in this book:

Action Images page 130; **Colorsport** pages 26, 66; **Getty Images** chapter title pages, pages 78, 111, 116, 136, 143, 157; **M&Y News Agency**, Portsmouth page 63; **Mirrorpix** pages 18 (Scottish Daily Record), 150; **PA Photos** pages 6–7, 10, 13, 21, 31, 33, 42, 47, 51, 57, 70, 75, 83, 88, 91, 94, 100, 105, 119, 124, 126, 132, 138, 146, 153, 158–9.